FIND IT   LEVERAGE IT IMPROVE IT PROFIT FROM IT

F.L.I.P. ™

The Ultimate Guide to SUCCESSFULLY invest in Real Estate

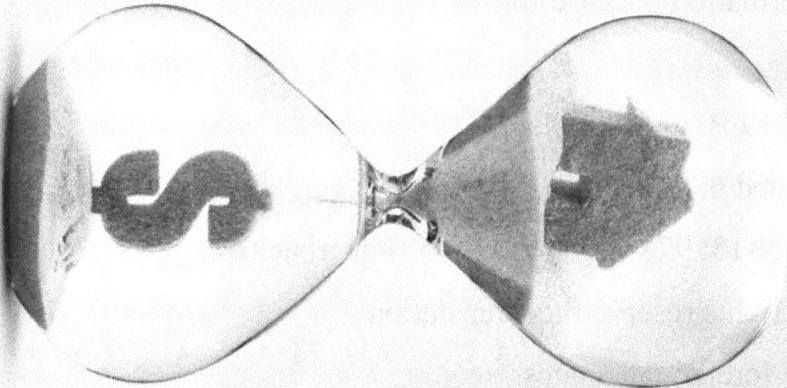

HOW TO MASTER THE FOUR KEY COMPONENTS OF EVERY SUCCESSFUL REAL ESTATE DEAL.

B. OCTAVIUS FAIR

©2019 B. Octavius Fair

Printed in the USA.

ISBN-13: 978-1-7331507-0-5 (Paperback)

All rights reserved for translation

into foreign languages.

F.L.I.P™

How to master the four key components of every SUCCESSFUL real estate deal

(How to) Find It

(How to) Leverage It

(How to) Improve It

(How to) Profit from It

By

B. Octavius Fair

Testimonials

Cher-Lewisville

I contacted B. Octavius on a Monday; within the week I had a wholesale property under contract. Property closed seven days later. $2000 fee was earned from working less than four hours total.

Demi-Chicago

I'm an airline transportation supervisor who makes $50k per year. I used B. Octavius' strategies and principles. I located a 3bedroom, 2bathroom, single-family residence (SFR). Bought and flipped the property within four months, net $65k.

Joel Garcia- Ft. Worth

I was just like you; I've watched the TV shows and heard about the different real estate workshops and seminars. I was still skeptical but curious. I bought into B. Octavius' system of wholesaling. Seven months later, I've made over $100k.

Table of Contents

CONNECT
WITH B. OCTAVIUS FAIR

SOCIAL MEDIA

BOCTAVIUS- FACEBOOK
BOCTAVIUS3247 - INSTAGRAM
@UNFAIRACADEMY - TWITTER

EMAIL INFO

BOCTAVIUS@BOCTAVIUS.COM
BOCTAVIUS@UNFAIRACADEMY.COM

WEBSITE

BOCTAVIUS.COM
UNFAIRACADEMY.COM

B. OCTAVIUS FAIR
REAL ESTATE INVESTOR   AUTHOR

What people Think	What I know
	Hard work, Dedication,
LUCK,	Preparation, sacrifice, studying
MORE LUCK	Disclipline Agressive, risk

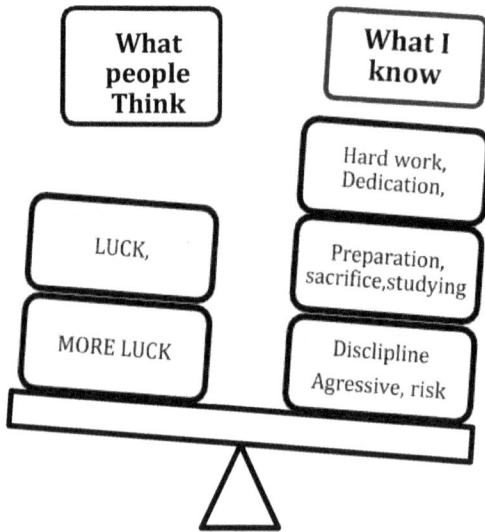

Let's Get Started

It is agreed; you bought this book to learn how to flip houses and to make serious money. Many would attest that the best way to achieve a goal is to write it down using the S.M.A.R.T. method for goal setting. I have an idea; let's make it fun.

Write down and take a picture of your goals using the S.M.A.R.T. method. Then, send me a message via e-mail at the following e-mail address: Boctavius@Boctavius.com. I'll hold you accountable and keep you motivated. I believe in you, so go ahead. Let's get started!

S.M.A.R.T. GOALS FOR INVESTING IN REAL ESTATE

B.OTAVIUS FAIR

S SPECIFIC	State your goals and answer these questions. "Why is it important to reach this Goal? What will reaching this goal do for you?"
M MEASURABLE	How will you be able to measure your progress? What steps need to happen on a weekly/monthly basis?
A ATTAINABLE	Can it be done? Is it achievable? Are your expectations aligned with the amount of work you are willing to invest to be successful?
R RELEVANT	Does this goal make reasonable sense? Is this goal the right time in your life?
T TIME-BOUND	When will you reach this goal. Be specific!
SIGNATURE, DATE & TIME	X——————————————————— ———————————————————— ————————————————————

DEDICATION

Dedication

If you believe like me, in the old African proverb, *"It takes an entire village to raise a child,"* this book is dedicated to all the men and women who invested in me as a young child. To my first pastor, Henry Wilkins IV, and the entire Highland Hills United Methodist Church family, without you, I am scared to think what I would have been. To the most inspiring entrepreneur of my lifetime, my father, Ruben B. Fair, though you are no longer here on earth, you live on through me and inspire me daily. To my eldest child, Octavia, and my youngest child, Matthew, I'm blessed, honored, and thankful that God has allowed you to call me Dad.

If you don't work on or continue to pursue your dream, you will end up working someone else's."

~Unknown

INTRODUCTION

INTRODUCTION

Ever since I was a child in Radcliff, Kentucky, it has always been my desire to matter in life. By matter, I mean that my presence on earth will have a lasting effect on everyone—anybody I meet would never forget me; anyone I encountered would know there was something unique, different, and intriguing about me; and, of course, like everyone else, I wanted to be very wealthy!

As I began to get older, it became more and more apparent to accomplish my goal of being very wealthy; I needed a platform from which to speak. I began to look at high net worth individuals and people of influence in the United States. This led me to start the ultimate soul search to find the "vehicle" (metaphorically), to help me achieve my goal. So, my quest began.

- Become a doctor? Nope, can't stand the sight of blood, and certainly wasn't the brightest student in biology.

- Become a lawyer? Three words. THE BAR EXAM. Oops, not me, wasn't the best at taking tests.

- Maybe be a Tech Junkie? Nope; not that either. I can't stand math past basic arithmetic.

The list goes on and on. Not so far down, however, I noticed a common theme… most of the wealthiest individuals in this country have a foundation in Real Estate. Then, the revelation hit; I can do Real Estate! Real Estate seems easy and has made more millionaires in this country than any other profession without a college degree.

As I contemplated the prospect of being in Real Estate, the first and most popular position came to mind… become a realtor. However, after my due diligence, I quickly figured out being a realtor wasn't for me. No offense to all the realtors out there; I applaud you for doing countless hours of digging for leads, listing houses, and finding bona fide buyers.

However, for me, there's just way too many hours invested with the outcome solely dependent upon the actions of others. I wanted to be in *total* control of my income, set my own hours, negotiate a price and, of course, collect a fat check. So, the next question was, *how*?

4

I dove headfirst into becoming a real estate wholesaler/investor, and, after much trial and error, I started to become successful. What did I do? How did I do it? Why was I so successful? Before now, I couldn't put it into words. I was so young (in Real Estate) and oblivious.

All I knew was that I was finding discounted properties, somehow coming up with the money to purchase them, improving the property, and then selling for a profit. Then, it dawned on me. I was doing the actual word F.L.I.P. (Finding it; Leveraging it; Improving it; and, Profiting from it.) Thus, the only title that would be fitting for this book is F.L.I.P.!

Best Time to Start

Now! There will never be "perfect timing;" it doesn't exist! Stop thinking it does and start the wheels of action in motion. You can do it! Procrastination ruins most of our future arrival plans. Being aggressive in seizing the moment is the difference between being wealthy or having a lifestyle of just barely getting by.

Rest assured, there are thousands upon thousands of people who have thought about investing in Real Estate because it sounds great, and the money seems to be amazing. Unfortunately, they never start! They never give themselves the slimmest of opportunity to enjoy the quality of life they envisioned their lives could be as a child.

I remember my father speaking to me shortly before his passing. He gave me an "ole skool" saying that has resonated in my innermost consciousness ever since. He said, *"No one is going to take care of the OLD YOU but the YOUNG YOU."* This revelation will forever be permanent in my spirit. I've grown up to know he was exactly right.

By investing in this book, you have made the same decision I made. You are not content in staying in the same socioeconomic place. Finally, there has been a realization that where you are today is not akin to where you thought you would be at this stage of your life. Moreover, to add "salt to your wounds"—to be completely honest—up until now, you probably didn't have a solid plan to get out of your current situation either.

With that said, if done correctly, this book can transform your life. Let's talk about the steps and processes of becoming a successful real estate investor. The only question now is, "Are you up for the challenge?"

> *"You might be poor, your shoes might be tattered and torn, but your mind is a palace."* -Frank McCourt

The Shifting of Your Mind

When I started my quest into Real Estate, I had to change a couple of things in my life. Realizing there were several things I had to accomplish, I had to prioritize them in the order I perceived to be relevant.

The first thing I had to change was my mentality. Regardless of your religious affiliation, if any, most of us can agree with the Bible when it says, "Be transformed by the *renewing* of your mind." If we are honest with ourselves, we can attest that making a paradigm shift of this magnitude begins in your mind.

In changing your mentality, we must dis-spell and debunk some of the myths that might hinder your mindset from completely going all-in with Real Estate investing.

1.   ***Making money in Real Estate is quick and easy.***

Wrong! Like everything else in life, anything worth having will not be quick or easy. The same is true in Real Estate. Yes, after gaining some knowledge and experience, over time, you will come to find it much more lucrative and certainly more profitable than the traditional 9-5 job. But, by no stretch of the imagination will this be quick and easy.

2.   ***You must be wealthy to invest in Real Estate.***

Wrong! Wholesaling makes it possible to get a property under contract at a set price; find an end-buyer(investor) to purchase at a higher price. Once the deal closes, the wholesaler makes the mark-up (generally between $7000-$10,000) with absolutely no money out of pocket.

3.   ***You need a lot of cash or have a high credit score.***

Wrong! Re-read #2; the same principle applies.

4.   ***It is very time-consuming.***

Wrong! What you put in is *exactly* what you'll get out. Real Estate is a unique market that allows you to make money passively or aggressively.

Who complains about making life- changing money? Let me answer that... *No one!* Usually, over time, the number of hours will begin to rack up, but so does the money (exponentially). What a trade-off! So again, who's complaining?

5. *Before you start, you must have a strong knowledge base of Real Estate.*

Wrong! Keep reading this book; you will be just fine. This book provides the foundation; the experience will come once you begin flipping houses.

6. *Flipping houses is just like it is on TV.*

Wrong! There are many more moving parts that *are not* shown on TV, probably because time doesn't allow for it. Indeed, there are some tedious aspects of real estate investing that aren't good for the Nielsen Rating. The marketing aspect of finding properties, the negotiating process in securing the property, setting up the legal entity, and actually going to Home Depot or your local hardware store—back and forth, up and down the aisle, ordering all the materials for the flip project— is boring.

9

So, no, flipping houses is not just like TV... TV is only a glorified portion of the portrait.

7. *The Real Estate market will always go up.*

Uh, oh... Wrong here, too! Notice the keyword *"Market,"* which would suggest somewhere supply and demand would play a role. There are two primary schools of thought. The first, *"What goes up, must come down"*, or the second, *"Buy it right, and it doesn't matter what the economy does"*. We subscribe to the latter.

> *"Everything you ever wanted, sits on the other side of fear."* -
> George Addair

Fear, for some reason, has a crippling effect and limits us from getting exactly what we want. When it pertains to trying something new, something challenging, or something no one else is doing, fear holds us back from stepping out to attempt that new frontier. However, the truth is, **"The money"** is on the other side of fear. You say, "I want a new car," then fear creeps in and says, "You can't afford one." You say, "I want a new house," then fear says, "Not too big, just in case I lose my job."

You say, "I want to start my own business," then doubt runs rampage through your mind and says, "You don't have enough time or money to devote to it."

Most of the time, fear beat us down, and thus defeats us before we can begin to start. Why does it have to be that way? *It doesn't!* Let's flip fear from a negative connotation into positive motivation. My knowledge and insight of Real Estate investing (yes, I'm bragging ;-) can help uproot any level of negative fear that would prohibit you from taking the first steps of Real Estate investing. From now on, your goal every day should be attempting to reach your maximum God-given potential. My pledge to you is to relay the key essential aspects of becoming a successful investor. The only question is, "Are you ready for the challenge?"

Teamwork Makes the Dream Work

By nature, and in general, we are more similar than different. Therefore, this statement reigns true for most of us. When starting a new journey or endeavor, most of us would prefer to begin by ourselves. Here is why. We want the self-gratification and all the success linked directly back to our actions and our tremendous business competence.

However, when starting something of this magnitude, it is very crucial to have seasoned Real Estate professionals willing to work on your behalf. In no way, by yourself, will you be able to go at it alone. The following are clear examples of what you will endure:

- *The Legal*– Have a trusted title company/lawyer to aid in the execution of the documents.

- *The Leveraging* – Have several bankers/hard money lenders available to see what they would loan out on the property. Most often, they are an excellent resource in knowing the actual ARV (After Repair Value).

- *The Improving* – Have a general contractor available and ready to review the scope of work.

Going at it alone is the absolute surest way to fail. Even if you tried to do it all by yourself, your time would be exasperated, and your results will be minimal.

<u>Notes</u>

01

SOLVING THE PROBLEM

01

Chapter 1: SOLVING THE PROBLEM

"You don't have to be rich to invest, but in order to be rich, you definitely must invest."

I've come to know your usefulness is only as great as the problems you can solve. I want to be useful to you; I want to solve your financial issues. Solving a problem ultimately starts with acknowledging and attacking the matter of contention. Let's state our dilemma:

- We are not earning enough money;

- We don't have enough time to do what we *really* want to do; and,

- Our financial future needs a shot in the arm.

One, if not all, of these statements, is the reason you have purchased this book and decided to metamorphose your current life status.

When solving a problem/dilemma, answering these three components are essential: "How, when, and why." The Real Estate industry is no different.

We have established to solve a problem, dilemma, or objective; we must ask ourselves, *"How, when, and why."* For the sake of this book, and a true "global" understanding of real estate investing, it would better serve us if we start in reverse order and ask *"Why, when, and how."*

Why Real Estate?

Real estate, done correctly, can produce the highest maximum return per dollar invested than any other investment vehicle. Where do most people traditionally invest their money? Let me answer that for you: stocks, bonds, gold, silver, commodities, and Certificate of Deposit. How do you buy them? That's easy, too—with money. Here is a scenario of Real Estate vs. other investment vehicles per dollar invested.

(Stay with me, you might need a notepad.)

Let's hypothetically say you have $100k to invest. If the stock prices are $100,000 per share, you will pay $100,000 per share for the ownership. You now own **one** share worth $100,000. A Certificate of Deposit (CD) is initially worth all the money you bring to the table. You deposit $100,000, and your CD initially is worth $100,000. In each case, it took **$100,000** to own 100% of that asset.

Here is why the ***power of Real Estate*** is so attractive. If you want to buy a small rental house that is move-in ready for the same $100,000. In most cases, you would only have to bring **10%** as a down payment, which equals **$10,000** to own **100%** of the asset.

Hypothetically, if the small rental house appreciated by 50%, your investment is now worth $150,000, of which the profit would be $50,000 or a whopping 500% return on your investment.

In the earlier stock example, using the same formula of appreciating by 50%, $100,000 x .50 = $150,000, or $50,000 profit. The key here is, in Real Estate, it only took **$10,000** to make **$50,000,** as opposed to **$100,000** to make $50,000 from other investments. Which one sounds better to you?

In Real Estate, less money is required to own the entire asset, which, in turn, means you can buy and own more assets than if you bought into other investment vehicles. But wait; it gets even better than that. To me, a *true* investment is an asset that does *two* things:

- It grows in capital value, **AND**

- It provides positive, passive cash flow throughout the life of ownership.

Question? Does a stock portfolio provide passive monthly income? *No!* Does a CD allow you to get paid off the interest monthly? Nope, not there either. However, does a rental property provide positive, passive cash flow? *Bingo!*

Now, do you see the power of real estate? My bad, I do apologize; that was the deepest I will go into math equations for the rest of the book. ;-) Promise, B. Fair

90/10/1 Formula

Real estate investing, in its true essence, has the components to be the perfect illustration for a formula to become successful in any business model, *regardless of the industry*.

The Almighty-90

Buy or Sell a product 90% of the population will need daily.

The housing market, which includes single-family residences, duplexes, and apartment complexes, makes up well over 90% of what everyone needs daily: ***Shelter***. It (shelter) has been here since the beginning of time; we all must have it, and it will never go "out of style"! So, why not be in an industry where the *demand* will always be in *demand?*

The Top Ten

Be in the top 10% of those who can provide to the 90%.

Great companies like Walmart, Chick-fil-A, and Amazon all succeed because they can provide their product to their respective 90% market. Just like them, you will need to develop advertising strategies that work.

Keep reading this book; our approaches and techniques can help shape a business model that will work within your current lifestyle. Working to be in the top 10% in your local market will solely depend on your hard work, tenacity, and dedication to achieving this goal. I believe you can, do you?

The Top One Percent

Just like in high school, the top 1% percent usually gets the most recognition. Being a successful real estate investor is no different. Be in the top 1% of those who can deliver the *goods* efficiently, affordably, and timely. Be considered the quintessential resource for information and product—the one to go to when people need whatever.

What makes this work in real estate investing? One word... *options!* As a real estate investor, you want options—options of different wholesalers, options in variant contractors, and options in various bankers. Having connections that are reliable and resourceful will ultimately build your brand and make your *product* (the houses you buy and sell) move along smoothly.

Be Decisive

While earning a bachelor's degree in business from Dallas Baptist University (DBU), my time there was full of fun—accompanied by many memorable events that have lasted thus far in my life. Meeting people from many different walks of life, gaining and sharing cultural experiences, and going through a rigid program of getting a "perceived" education has had a lasting effect on who I am today.

But, to be brutally honest, passing the 128 credit hours required, spending innumerable hours in the classroom, followed by countless hours of studying, I hate to say it, but, I have forgotten most of the principles of the application associated with the coursework. This is especially true in algebra, biology, and chemistry. (Probably you, too. Try reading your high school sophomores' chemistry book, and you will see what I mean.) Ha Ha!

However, of the 1% remembered, there is one sentence from business school that has stuck with me thus far in my life. It stays at the forefront of my business mental hard drive. I use it frequently. It's a constant reminder and motivator. Whenever my mind begins to wonder, doubt, or second guess a *well*-thought-out plan; I use it. Here it is…

"More money has been lost due to *indecision,* as opposed to the *wrong decision*."

"Corporate America" uses this philosophy every day. "Corporate America" is not ashamed, afraid, or timid about spending millions of dollars on a new ad campaign, slogan, or phase. If the ad is successful, it keeps getting ran. If it's a total flop, it gets pulled, and they move on to the next. The point is *to be decisive.* Don't mull around in doubt, procrastination, or fear, playing the "what if" game. Always be producing something, always striving to reach a goal, be that person who "tips the scale"—the leader that was born inside of you.

Yeah, yeah, yeah. But you say, "Corporate America has millions upon millions of dollars of revenue, and I don't." Guess what? That's exactly how they got it—by being aggressive, seizing the moment/opportunity, and a *well*-thought-out plan of execution. Being decisive, dynamic, and having a well thought out game plan are also the fundamental components in being a *successful* real estate investor.

Real estate cannot be lost or stolen, nor can it be carried away. Purchased with common sense, pay in full, and managed with reasonable care, it is about the safest investment in the world-

Franklin D. Roosevelt

02

WHOLESALING

02

Chapter 2: WHOLESALING

WARNING:

Reading this section may increase your sense of urgency fivefold. Stop, turn, and run now if you don't want to make millions.

I am sure most people who purchased this book are still wondering how you can make thousands upon thousands of dollars with no money down or without using your own money. It seems like a gimmick—too good to be true— yet, it's done every hour of every day.

First, it is essential to know and understand why I, and so many of my students, have been so successful in real estate investing. We have realized to sustain a lasting career as a real estate investor, the following principle must remain at the forefront. It is this:

To learn how to reduce your time spent working while increasing the money you earn.

It seems like an incredible principle—fabulous and a pure stroke of genius. However, in a traditional workforce setting, rarely, if ever, is this accomplished. Imagine if you went into your boss's office and said, "My new hours are 9:00 a.m. to 12:45 p.m., Monday through Thursday, with Fridays off, same salary!" Imagine the response. Let me answer it, "You're *fired*." But, oh, if we could all accomplish this feat, wouldn't life be that much more enjoyable? You would see places you always dreamt, spend more time with the kids, and probably give back volunteering to your favorite local charity. Wouldn't life seem so much more complete?

Now, here's your chance—wholesaling Real Estate. It is perfect for those who consider themselves a *people person*—one who loves negotiating and doesn't like getting their hands dirty. Hmmm, that sounds just like me!

Real Estate wholesaling is finding a motivated seller and securing the house under contract. The next action is to find an investor and assign that contract to them at a higher price. Once the property sells, you collect the difference of the mark up in price. Here is the illustration below.

WHOLESALING FIGURE EXAMPLE 1 A	
ARV (After Repair Value)	$200,000
Repair Cost	- $20,000
Misc., Closing Cost, Title Policy	-$10,000
Total	$170,000
Of the $170,000 most investors like to be at 70% max leverage	
Investor	$170,000 x 70%
Max Purchase Price	$ 119,000
Contract Price	$105,000
Wholesalers Profit	+14,000

(I am giving you credit now as already being a wholesaler. Congratulations!)

A typical wholesaling transaction would look like this: The perceived ARV is $200,000. The wholesaler (you) can secure the contract for $105,000. In your estimation, the property needs $20,000 in repairs. The wholesaler finds an investor to buy the property at $119,000. The wholesaler assigns the contract to a said investor. The wholesaler makes a $14,000 profit.

Wow, it is just that simple! To be very clear, wholesaling is flipping, except the time frame is substantially shorter, there are no repairs, and the wholesaler never actually purchases the property. Wholesaling eliminates the financial risk, time spent on the renovation, and of course, the carrying costs that accrue throughout the life of the rehab project.

We have established what is wholesaling; Now, it is essential to lay a foundation of some fundamental rules. Don't get too *spoiled*; earning $3,000-$20,000 per transaction does require discipline and some work. Look at the following:

Know What You Are Wholesaling

- Go inside.
- Inspect the property.
  - Know the age of the roof and the A/C unit.
  - Know the quality of the entire electrical system.
  - Know about any foundation and plumbing issues.

2. **Location, Location, Location** – Know your market. As a wholesaler, you should know the "Three Locations" of the property.

   - **Location #1** – The name of the city. (i.e., South of Interstate 35, in a small town called Timbuctoo.)

   - **Location #2** – The sub-division the property sits in within the city. (i.e., Cobblestone Crest addition or Silver Creek addition)

   - **Location #3** – The block where the house sits within the sub-division. (i.e., Corner lot, behind the church, next to a field, facing south.)

3. **Take Plenty of Pictures** – This will eliminate the constant viewing of the property by other investors. It will also save you time/effort and, more importantly, it will not disturb the tenants of the home. Many investors gauge their interest and price point by pictures alone. Pictures of the kitchen, bathroom, A/C unit, and the water heater can tell the story of the entire house. It can speak volumes to a seasoned investor; my advice would be to take at least 30 pics.

4. **Keep the "Main Thang" the "Main Thang"** – The single most important job of a wholesaler is finding *great deals.* Period, T*he End!*

For those of you who slightly want to get your hands dirty and dibble and dabble into the world of rehabbing a project, there is a middle of the road real estate investment tool between wholesaling and a total rehab flip. I like to call it **"Mini-Max Wholesale Flip".**

Mini-Max Wholesale Flip

Mini-Max Wholesale Flip's definition, according to B. Octavius Fair, is *doing very little work on the property to get the maximum wholesale amount from that property.* This process would involve fixing up the appearance of the property by taking up the floors, removing old fixtures, the disposal of old appliances, throwing away trash, cutting the grass, and trimming trees. Doing this will provide a clear open view of the entire property.

Therefore, giving the investor(s) a clean slate as they walk through the property to see precisely what they're about to own. On average, this bumps the sale price 12-15% higher. However, it does require ownership of the property.

Here are some added *Keys to Success*. This will aid in the development and stability of your wholesaling business.

1. Don't worry about not making the same money as if you were to do a full renovation; it's the volume that counts, how many and how fast.

2. Always add a contingency to the contract allowing you to back out of the deal, if for some unforeseen reason, you are unable to find an end buyer before the closing date.

3. Offer as little as possible for the option money and earnest money to secure the contract with the seller.

4. Always collect an earnest money deposit from your end buyer. No exceptions. I mean, ***no exceptions!***

5. $2,000 should be your minimum earnest money accepted from the end buyer. The $2000 is due at the SIGNING of the contract with the end buyer.

6. Never accept a personal check as a form of payment for earnest money from your end buyer. I don't have to explain; I'm sure if you bought this book, you are bright enough to know you need certified funds.

7. There are "fortunes" in the follow-up! Even if you make an offer to a seller at $110,000, but the seller wants $130,000. Unfortunately, there's no agreement; therefore, no contract. But that's okay! Continue to follow up with the seller, even though an initial agreement was unable to be reached. Keeping in contact builds rapport, shows commitment, and keeps you fresh on the seller's mind. You just never know; the motivation for selling may have changed since last you spoke. There could been a death in the family (heaven forbid), an incarceration, or a pending foreclosure; you just never know, and you would never have known if you didn't follow up. Always follow up. Let me say that again; *always follow up*—until the home sells to you (hopefully) or someone else. Michelle Moore said it best, "Not following up with your potential sellers is like filling up your bathtub without first putting the stopper in the drain."

8. Build your list of buyers (investors). Always keep increasing the "pool of applicants" (better known as investors) to your business. One of the worst feelings ever, and indeed the quickest way to get frustrated, is to invest and to employ many man-hours in locating and getting a wholesale property under contract; then having to back out of the deal because there is not an investor willing to purchase your wholesale deal. What a waste of time, energy, and lost earning potential! I can't express how, under no circumstance, should this ever be you. Have a list of investors ready to go and continue to check in with them—albeit by email or text message—at least once every 10 to 15 days to make sure they are still on board and ready to purchase.

Wholesaling real estate can fix a lot of financial ills, such as cash flow problems, high credit card balances, and overdue bills. Here's how. Remember the $2000 earnest money? *It's non-refundable!* (Of course, put it in the contract). Whether the investor closes on the deal or not, at minimum, $2000 was earned.

Question? Would $2,000 take care of an electricity bill or two? Now, do you see why it is exponentially important to have investors ready to purchase?

Wholesaling Recap

1.   Time – Wholesaling saves a whole lot of it.

2.   Money – Wholesaling doesn't need any.

3.   Labor – Wholesaling requires a tremendous amount, but it's not manual.

4.   No Rehab – When wholesaling there is no need to worry about color schemes, countertops, or flooring ideas. You are not planning to own nor reside in the home.

5. Fast Liquidity – Wholesaling yields a quick return on investment.

6. Less Risk – Wholesaling decreases your risk to financial exposure.

7. No Red Tape – The end buyers are usually investors, meaning all-cash buyers without rules and restrictions from banks.

Ever wonder what happened to the "P.S." when ending a letter to someone? Did it go out of style? Is it extinct? For this section, I'm going to bring back the *ole skool* "P.S."

To: You the Potential Real Estate Mogul

From: B. Octavius Fair

Society has conditioned our mindset to believe in the value of a strong work ethic. Although having a strong work ethic has its merits, often it has a hindering effect. **"What you talkin' 'bout, Willis?"** *(in my Gary Coleman voice. Those who grew up in the 1980's would understand).*

Those who subscribe to the theory of a strong work ethic surmise, **"I go to work every day; I never miss a day. I work long hours, and I work hard. Therefore, I have a very strong**

37

work ethic." Yet, they are broke before months' end and can't figure out why.

Here's why. Usually, the people who say they have a strong work ethic forget about the principles of a smart work ethic. Here's my smart work ethic principle:

"Spending the least amount of time, making the same (if not greater) income, will equal more opportunity to repeat the process."

Now, that's smart! Most of the time, working smart outweighs a strong work ethic. Done right, wholesaling will achieve a smart work ethic.

Remember, never waste time; unlike water, it's a commodity that can never be replenished. *-B. Octavius Fair*

Smart Work Ethic Personified

WHOLESALING	VS.	FLIPPING
AVERAGE PROFIT		**AVERAGE PROFIT**
$5000		$52,5000
AVERAGE HOURS SPENT		**AVERAGE HOURS SPENT**
10		720
AVG TIME BEFORE COLLECTING PROFIT		**AVG TIME BEFORE COLLECTING PROFIT**
14 DAYS		85 DAYS
AVG. AMOUNT OF FINANCIAL RISK		**AVG. AMOUNT OF FINANCIAL RISK**
$0		$185,000
CHANCES TO COMPLETE PER QUARTER		**CHANCES TO COMPLETE PER QUARTER**
UNLIMITED		1
AVG. MADE PER HOUR		**AVG. MADE PER HOUR**
$500		$72.91

> *There are risks and costs to action. However,*
> *they are far less than the long-range risks of*
> *comfortable inaction.* -John F. Kennedy

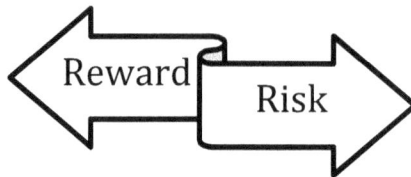

Risky Business

I get it; most people are scared to invest in real estate because of the risk. They are afraid to lose those precious hard-earned dollars earned from putting in long hours playing the "Climbing the Corporate Ladder" game. From the left side of the brain (rational thinking side for the non-biology majors), it has been programmed in their minds to think it is either all or nothing when it comes risk.

Ever heard of the phrases, "No guts, no glory," or "No pain, no gain"? What about, "You gotta risk it, to get the biscuit?" These phrases imply some truth, but not all. Yes there are *calculated* risks involved in real estate investing.

To be completely transparent, I am the true classic definition of a risk-averse person. Risk averseness is all down in my bones. However, as a real estate investor, I do everything in my reasonable power to eliminate all (or certainly reduce) the amount of risk and create avenues where Certainty (as a proper noun) can reside.

I've come to know risk and real estate go hand-in-hand. It (the risk) can never be avoided entirely or eliminated; it must be managed. Here is how I manage risk: It encourages me to seek more information, to ask more questions, and to be more diligent in my "global" research of the project. Once the assessment is complete, I have uncovered the risk. Now, I'm ready to start making money flipping properties

<u>**NOTES**</u>

03

FIND IT

03

F

F

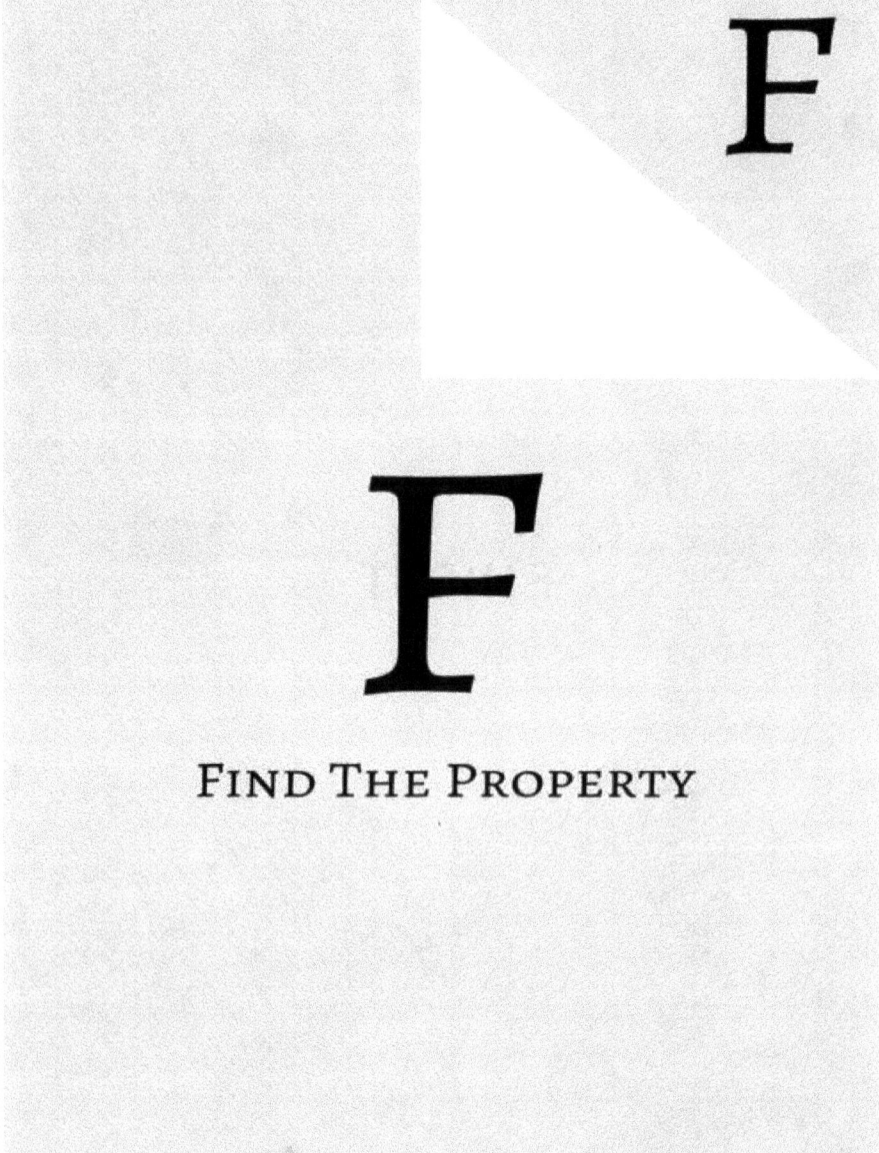

FIND THE PROPERTY

Chapter 3: FINDING THE PROPERTY

> *"If you really want to do something, you will find a way. If you don't, you will find an excuse."*
>
> ### *Jim Rohn*

If you are at this stage of the book, I am convinced you are ready to begin your real estate investing career. No doubt, I want you to be successful, and my job to provide information the road of least resistance. Remembering the purpose of this book is to provide optimum success for the beginner or intermediate real estate investor, once you become seasoned, feel free to expound on these parameters for finding discounted homes and motived sellers.

Qualifying your search

"Where do I find properties that qualify?"

"Qualify?"

"Yes, Qualify!"

Simply finding properties that are at, or either slightly

below, market prices is useless. The goal is to buy extremely low and change the comps (higher of course) when selling. We need distressed properties, inherited unwanted estates, and motivated sellers.

Please note, the qualifying standards/parameters are slightly different if the goal is to fix and flip, as opposed to wholesale, but for the most part, they are the same. Here are the preliminary standards/parameters.

- Purchase most of your homes that are in favorable living conditions; and,

- Buy homes with at least 30%-35% of the equity.

**Value of
your Home**   **Amount Owed
on your Mortgage**   **Home
Equity**

Identifying Target Investment Properties

Your local marketplace will undoubtedly have properties that have the wrong things wrong with them. Homes with outdated floor plans that require an additional bathroom, bedrooms, or a garage to bring them up to date are functional obsolescence. Eliminate these homes from investment consideration. Homes with extensive roof damage, severe foundation problems, previously flooded, or have/had severe mold and asbestos issues should not be considered for investment either.

Just as important as the type of homes that qualifies, greater distinction is placed on the *type* of neighborhoods. On the following page are some characteristics of neighborhoods that are "worth the worth." Most of the criteria for the "characteristics of the neighborhood" needs little to no explanation, except this one: Expensive Neighborhoods.

It is a given there are individual states/cities where higher-priced homes are the norm—California, New York City, and Washington D.C., to name a few.

Show me the Money!
(Neighborhoods Qualifying Characteristics)

AGE OF NEIGHBORHOOD QUALIFIES

Homes at least 20-35 yrs. old

AGE OF NEIGHBORHOOD DISQUALIFIES

Homes that are new construction,
Homes that are<10 yrs old
Homes that are over 60 yrs old

Condition of Home

No foundation problems
No structural problems
Roof condition relatively good
Limited external damage-gutters-paint

Characteristic of an ideal neighborhood

Middle class
Low crime rate shopping mall,
school, church<.7.5 miles miles away
Most of the residents are over 45 years of age
An apartment complex is not adjacent
Expensive neighborhood-No, No, I mean NO!!
Most recent sales show neighborhood values are rising.

To me, *expensive* is a relative word. In this case, it is relative to the metropolitan area. Staying away from the homes where the upper middle class and the elite reside are the type of neighborhood I am referencing.

I know; I know; I know. The opportunity to potentially make a 6-figure payday by renovating a very expensive home in a costly neighborhood may seem like an excellent business opportunity/investment. However, to me, it's not. Here is why:

Higher Acquisition Costs – Origination fees, title insurance, and down payments will be significantly higher. The example below is a typical hard money loan.

HARD MONEY LOAN		
COST TO CLOSE TYPICAL VS EXPENSIVE NEIGHBORHOOD HOME		
LOAN AMOUNT	$175,000	$700,000
ORIGINATION (2%)	$3,500	$14,000
DOWN PAYMENT (10%)	7,500	$70,000
TITLE INSURANCE (1%)	$1,700	$6,000
COST TO CLOSE	$22,700	$84,700

Rehab Costs – Usually, these homes are larger than the typical single-family residence, which would suggest more materials will be needed; thus, equaling higher materials cost.

On average, these homes require a higher grade of material. Authentic hardwood flooring and marble in bathrooms to facilitate the taste buds of the pickiest of buyers are usually required.

More Expensive Carrying Costs – The mortgage, taxes, and insurance are insanely more expensive. These costs can eat at or up the potential profit in a matter of months.

Days on the Market Are Longer – Houses like these often stay on the market longer. These factors are to include, but are not limited to, at least these two things:

- First, the "pool" of applicants buying this type of home is vastly smaller than average; and,

- Second, buyers at this level can buy anywhere in the metroplex; therefore, they are usually more sophisticated regarding the demands of the house.

Houses in These Neighborhoods Don't Come Around Too Often – It's harder to price homes in expensive neighborhoods due to the limited amount of sold comps in the immediate area. Because of this fact, sometimes realtors miscalculate the asking price. Consequently, after weeks on the market, a price reduction is warranted.

If indeed a price reduction is needed, a simple $5000 price reduction won't do. It will require a cut of $50,000, or even $100,000, to attract a new buyer. Can you say *ouch* to the bottom line?

> *The late great Elbert Hubbard uttered,* *"Every man is a d@m# fool for at least five minutes every day; wisdom consists in not exceeding that five minutes."*

I've been in the real estate investment community for quite some time, and many investors have gone against this principle. Over that time, I've come to notice this to be true: The ROI (Return on Investment) on expensive homes in expensive neighborhoods are usually not as high as returns on smaller homes; especially, given the amount of exposure to financial risk. On expensive homes, my advice to you would be to tread lightly and at your own risk.

51

Where the Value Lies

After searching for the neighborhood(s) that may qualify, you've finally landed on several in your metroplex that meets the above criteria. Remember, undervalued properties are essential.   Therefore, when searching within these neighborhoods, look for these types of properties.

Distressed Properties – A distressed property is a property in pre-foreclosure or being sold by the lender. A distressed property is a direct result of negligence on the part of the homeowner not paying the mortgage payments and/or tax bill on the property. As a result, in most cases, they usually don't keep up with routine maintenance, and the property is in a deplorable condition.

Motivated Sellers – There is a small distinction between a motivated seller and distressed properties. With a motivated seller, the issue here is timing. The seller may have a pending divorce, loss of a job, company relocation, or even a death in the family. Although the house could still be in foreclosure, it is usually not in poor condition.

Heirs – A person legally entitled to the property after the death of the predecessor; a person who is inheriting and *continuing* the legacy of the predecessor. This is my favorite. Notice, I put the second definition as well. The reasoning behind this is, often, the heir is *not* interested in carrying out the legacy of the deceased by using the property as a homestead. They are usually considerably younger and have nothing "invested" in the property.

By the heir not having "sweat equity" in the property (i.e., making payments, solving maintenance issues, and the all-important sentimental value), it makes it easier to part ways at a lower, more beneficial, price to you. The negotiations are much quicker and seamless.

Vacant Homes – Properties that are unoccupied and/or abandoned. Here is a great time to serve the community. Finding an empty/abandoned home is a great way to turn a community liability into a real asset. Vacant homes are usually an eyesore to the community. National studies have suggested a slight increase in drug and crime rates in communities where there are several vacant properties. Usually, these properties are owned by heirs. (Remember, we love them!) Finding these owners will require a little research and due diligence but, trust me on this, it will be well worth it. Some of my biggest wholesale flips have come from this source.

Advertising for Real Estate

Great, we now know *what we want*. Now it's time for what we want *to find us*. How? Glad you ask! By Advertising. Advertising does a multitude of things:

1. Advertising introduces a new product,
    2. Increase sales,
        3. Educates the consumer,

These things are essential for sure; however, there is one more component advertising does: It ELIMINATES THE MIDDLEMAN. Advertising establishes a direct line of communication between the manufacturer(you) and the consumer (the seller). When this link is connected, two things move in concert: Higher profits for you, AND a higher selling price for your consumer. Remember, in Real Estate investing, the name of the game is enormous profits and big fat checks.

Effective advertising can help you supersede your expectations. Now, let's perfect the art of advertising!!

The Four Lane Superhighway

Advertising is a super four-lane highway to let people know about your business. To make this "Highway," an effective medium of transport, requires thought and execution with the mindset of the customer at the forefront. Yes, you must promote, let me repeat, YOU MUST PROMOTE!!!

However, just promoting by itself is not the most vital element. You need "Quality" in your promotion. What makes the perfect Ad? One word, "Impact." The impact of your message should span throughout all your ad platforms. From foreclosure letters, bandit signs, door hangers, social media posts, or just simple personal marketing, the message should always be clear, concise, and with a purpose.

> *A great ad should make you think, talk about it, or at least do a double take.*
>
> **-B Octavius Fair**

Digging into the mindset of your customer

Over the years of investing, I have come to know this fact to be true. Your target audience doesn't care about your name, your title, your looks, your height, your weight, or status. They only care about **WHAT YOU CAN DO FOR THEM!** They are, in a sense, selfish. So, give them precisely what their emotional physic wants; Great headlines and attention-grabbing ads!!

There are many different styles of ad writing that will help you accomplish this goal. To me, here are the most effective.

1. Be Direct-We buy houses
2. Dictate a decree-Sell me your house!
3. Ask an interrogative question- Want to sell your house fast?

Your presentation of your ad will make people ultimately chose you over the competition. Remember, the race is very competitive when it comes to getting a chance to be in front of a motivated seller. The way you brand and build your promotion is the key to successfully finishing on top.

How to find the Jewels?

Bandit Signs – Are usually 24x24 and are used as a marketing tool to promote your real estate business. They should be suggestive and direct to the point. They should read like this:

> *WE BUY HOUSES. WE PAY ALL*
> *CLOSING.* WE CLOSE IN *7 DAYS.*
> *(214) 555-1234*

What I've found to be most effective are one-sided, two-color signs. Of course, it's your personal preference, but remember, my goal here is to provide the path of least resistance. To get real traction, order at least 100. Don't just place them anywhere; be strategic. Place them in neighborhoods where you desire to own or flip properties.

Also, drive through different neighborhoods to find the perfect spot visible for traffic. While you are driving, be on the lookout for vacant homes; we've already stated their importance. Word of caution, in some municipalities, it may be illegal to place signs in the medians of busy intersections, my advice would be to check first. Bandit Signs work! Let me repeat... ***Bandit Signs work!*** They should be a staple in your marketing plans and your budget. In other words, get a supply of them, be creative, and watch your phone ring off the hook with motivated sellers ready to do business.

WE BUY HOUSES
012-345-6789

30/30/300 Rule

Realtors – Remember the smart work ethic? (Ref Chapter 2, section P.S.) Here is another way to improve your real estate investing career efficiency rate. **The 30/30/300 Rule**. It is simple and should be utilized at least every 30 days. Every **30** days call **30** different realtors in your local area, relay to them who you are, what you do, and how you do it.

The conversation should go like this: *"Hello, my name is B. Octavius. I am a local investor in your city. I would like to be on your PRE-MLS investor list for those properties that require a private listing, quick sale, or are in poor condition that won't qualify for traditional lending. I can close in 3-5 days pending title work, all cash, no appraisal, and no inspection."*

Thirty realtors, if they are doing their job correctly, encounter at least 10 people per week who are selling their property under a distressing situation. My mother used to say, "The early bird gets the worm." By getting there first, you are eliminating most of the potential competition and subsequently avoiding bidding wars.

Realtors, for the most part, are very intelligent people, they know the value of a cash investor to their business model. If the realtor can get a buyer at his client's asking price *before* it is listed, they can potentially make the full commission of 6%. Furthermore, realtors who have been in business for a reasonable period of time know a lot can go wrong between the time the contract is signed and the final closing/funding of the deal. The security of knowing the deal won't fall through because of funding issues, or credit surprises at the end, adds a favorable position in doing business with you.

Additionally, here is the most important aspect—drum roll please—the realtor will receive the commission in 5-7 days as opposed to the normal 30-45 days in a traditional bank-financed transaction! Talk about a smart work ethic on *both ends;* it's a true win-win. The math says: 30 Realtors encounter 10 people; 30 x10 = 300. All you need is one; I certainly like those odds.

Notice of Default

Notice of Default (NOD) is a public notice filed with a court clerk's office stating a mortgage borrower has defaulted on a loan. The NOD is a public record. To me and you, it means pre-foreclosure, as it is the beginning stages of the foreclosure process. When the NOD is served, the borrower is at least two months behind.

The Notice of Default shows the name, address, and why they are in default. Most often, it is sent certified mail to ensure receipt. Here's how aggressive real estate investors turn NOD's into cash. NOD's are the perfect way to stay ahead of the competition curb. Remember, the less competition, the higher the success rate.

Often, the delinquent borrower may want to sell earlier in the foreclosure process rather than later, as they have no intention of reinstating the loan. *What an opportunity!* Most people like doing business with people with whom they have rapport. You have at least two month's head start on those investors who strictly use the foreclosure list. I'll see you at the county clerk's office!

Auction

Think about this. What does it take for a property to get to Auction? Eight to twelve months of non-payments, countless letters from the banks, hundreds of letters from those who have minded the NOD's, and multitudinous mailed letters from investors who use the foreclosure list. People are bold nowadays, so I'm also assuming 50 personal knocks on the homeowners' door.

If there was a lot of equity in the property, wouldn't the homeowner have at least tried to sell it to the previous 200 suitors? I'm not totally against auctions; however, as a young investor/new business, finding properties at the auction is not where a stable business model should rest—the auction is my least favorite option to build a lasting book of business.

Foreclosure list

Sifting through the foreclosure list has some value. A foreclosure list is just what it says. It includes the name, address of the property, and the amount delinquent. The foreclosure list also has the actual date of sale. Just remember, you are probably a month or two behind those investors who minded the NOD's and have probably contacted the delinquent owners. There is also added competition from nation-wide investing companies because this list can be purchased.

However, there is a chance the owner of these properties ignored the solicitations of companies using the NOD's. It may have taken a while for reality to sink in that this foreclosure process is real. They are now ready to do business pertaining to this matter. For properties that are on the foreclosure list, you should send a letter that reads like the one on the following page.

"Keep this letter! Do not throw it away!"

Hello, (Insert Homeowner's Name)

I received information about a "Notice of Default" from your bank; however, I'm thinking that you are wanting to catch up on your loan and continue living in your property. If so, we can help you!

ABSOLUTELY NO MONEY OUT OF YOUR POCKET!

We can stop the foreclosure process in as little as four days. Try us! What do you have to lose? One phone call to our office puts you one step closer to relieving the pain, stress, and uncertainty.

(Insert Your Name)
Sr. Foreclosure Strategy Consultant

P.S. If you are looking to sell your home, we can and we will buy any property, in any condition.

CALL TODAY! TIME IS OF THE ESSENCE.

PHONES ARE ANSWERED 24 HOURS A DAY, 7 DAYS A WEEK.

Office Number:
Fax Number:

Whatever you do, hold onto this letter and let us help you!

Paid Per Lead Generated List

Most counties now have a website where you can readily find information and the legal description of every property in that county. It is usually called the Central Appraisal District of said county. What makes technology so advantageous to investors? It's the ease of access. One of my favorite ways to source new investment properties comes from lists generated by a listing source agency. It is a pay per lead generated system. Here's how it works.

When a property is purchased as a homestead, the mailing address recorded on the deed is the same as the homestead address. However, when a property is purchased as an investment property, the mailing address is usually different. I'm guessing the owner probably would not prefer his/her mail going to tenants. The pay per lead company can run a database search with the criteria of "homestead and mailing addresses that are different." What the system comes back with is a list of all "absentee owners" in that county. What does that mean to you? Absentee owner is another word for "landlord."

Now, you have a list of landlords in the county of your search. Send them letters and or postcards. By chance, they may be "fed up" and tired of being a landlord or have a change in circumstances preventing them from keeping up with the maintenance of the property. They may be interested in selling a house individually or the entire rental portfolio. Who knows? Your job is to stay in touch; remember this old saying, "Birds of a feather flock together." If they are not interested in selling their home, they may know other people (friends/landlords) who are.

Wholesaling Companies

A real estate investment company is one whose sole purpose is to find distressed properties and motivated sellers to flip the contract to investors. The wholesaling company makes a profit (usually 10-20%) from the markup; they never actually own the property.

Using a wholesaling company as a source of finding motivated sellers and distressed properties is a quick and easy solution that should only be utilized by an advanced flipper. The ARV's (After Repair Values) stated by these companies are usually unattainable for newbie investors to reach, due to limited flipping experience. Remember the markup; you are essentially paying the "middleman" 10%-20% more than usual had the property been found on the foreclosure list, NOD's, auction, or from bandit signs.

Also, keep in mind, if it is an outstanding deal, there will be stiff competition from other investors whose pockets and repair resources are far deeper than yours. My advice would be to stay away as a young investor, but as experience grows, if you must, remember to tread with caution and do extensive research before purchasing.

YOUR GAME, YOUR RULES!

There are several different avenues and strategies that work in finding discounted homes and motivated sellers. Your job is to find your nitch, dig a ditch, and you will be rich. .-B.Octavius Fair

---

The UnFair Academy

Yes, I'm proud as a peacock to say it. The UnFair Academy leads are incredible. Sign up and join our family; we would love to have you. We can surely make this journey much smoother. Here is the link to subscribe: http://www.unfairacademy.com.

Now What?

Great! Simply awesome! You have found a house that meets the preliminary standards and parameters from a seller in a distressed situation. *Now what?* Your mind is probably running rampant with questions like:

- "How do I approach the seller?"
- "What do I say to the seller?"
- "What do I offer the seller?"
- Or, quite simply, "How do I close the deal?"

All great questions! The answering of each is as vital as the air you breathe. Calm down and take a deep breath. Getting the seller to "open up" about their home is simpler than you might think.

68

Before you begin on how to approach the seller, it is a given that you would greet him/her with a great smile, also stating your name and the name of your company. (Duh!) When approaching the seller of all the potential information that needs to be shared, there are two critical informational items to uncover that are most vital: **Motivation** and **Flexibility**.

It is your job to uncover the events that led to the circumstances that have caused the seller to become motivated to sell. From here, all questions and answers that arise will help to shape the rest of the conversation and, subsequently, your formal offer.

Asking the right types of questions is vital when building rapport and holding a productive conversation. During the fact-finding process, the discussion should flow freely and as normal as the typical "water cooler" conversation in a traditional workplace.

Stay away from close-ended questions, but instead use open-ended questions that require thought and authentic dialogue. Here are two examples:

- **Close-ended question:** How much are you selling your property for?
- **Open-ended question:** How did you arrive at the price point for the selling of your home?
- **Closed-ended question:** How old is the roof?
- **Open-ended question:** When was the last time the roof was replaced and why?

Both open-ended questions give you more informational ammunition to begin the process of forming your offer. You will need every ounce of information to aid in the reduction of the price.

Practice, *practice*, **practice** your presentation. Delivering an excellent fact-finding interview is a skill; like any other craft, it needs to be cultivated and refined.

The Offer

It is a foregone conclusion that every deal is unique, and there is no "one size fits all" model for submitting an offer. Because of the different personalities and circumstances involved, it is almost impossible to give instructions on what works best. However, there is a blueprint

I use on every seller that usually ensures, at the very least, the seller considers my offer.

The Mindset of a Full-time Buyer – Have the mindset of a full-time buyer against a part-time seller. Show leadership in presenting the offer. Give data reports on the house, stats of the neighborhood, and overall metropolitan trends. Remind the seller you continuously analyze the particulars of said community. It won't hurt to reiterate the fact you buy and sell real estate all day, every day. Doing this will establish credibility as the quintessential professional—one to be respected and trusted in this situation.

Offer All Cash – I offer all cash for at least two purposes: certainty and speed. You may have heard of the phrase, "Cash is King," right? But, did you know, it also has a calming effect on the negotiations with the seller? It gives the seller the assurance the deal will not have any hang-ups due to bank stipulations, regulations, appraisals, or inspections. Cash also provides the seller with confidence—pending title work, the deal will be sealed in seven days or less.

Get Something in Return – Never give in to a concession without getting something. Due to the emotions and the fear of losing the deal, most investors are afraid to use the word **"No."** Here is a solution. If the seller wants a leaseback, instead of saying, "No," offer a lower purchase price. If the seller wants more time to close, ask for owner financing. If the seller refuses to pay for title policy, insist they pay for the survey. *The bottom-line is don't concede without getting something in return.* You will be surprised at how well this works.

Maximum Purchase Price – When presenting the offer, have the maximum purchase price you are willing to offer ingrained in your mind. Of course, begin significantly lower, but not too low as this may offend the seller.

Always be Prepared to Walk Away – Sometimes, the best deal is the deal you **don't make**. Remember, you've done the research. You've put in hours upon hours of analyzing data of the neighborhood, and you have reviewed the potential closing costs, mortgage, taxes, insurance, and carrying costs. For the last couple of days, you have been going back and forth in your mind on the maximum purchase price. If the offer is not ***accepted***—at or better than that number—***walk away!*** There's no sense in investing in a deal that will waste a lot of time, energy, and effort. This is totally absurd. You must realize that, ultimately, this deal is counterproductive to your business model, which is to ***make money***.

Let logic rule the day.

Always buy on logic. It supersedes emotion, gut-feelings, or anxiousness. Logic is supported by data, facts, and trends from multiple sources. Emotion and gut- feelings are supported only by you.-B. Octavius Fair

<u>NOTES</u>

04

LEVERAGING IT

04

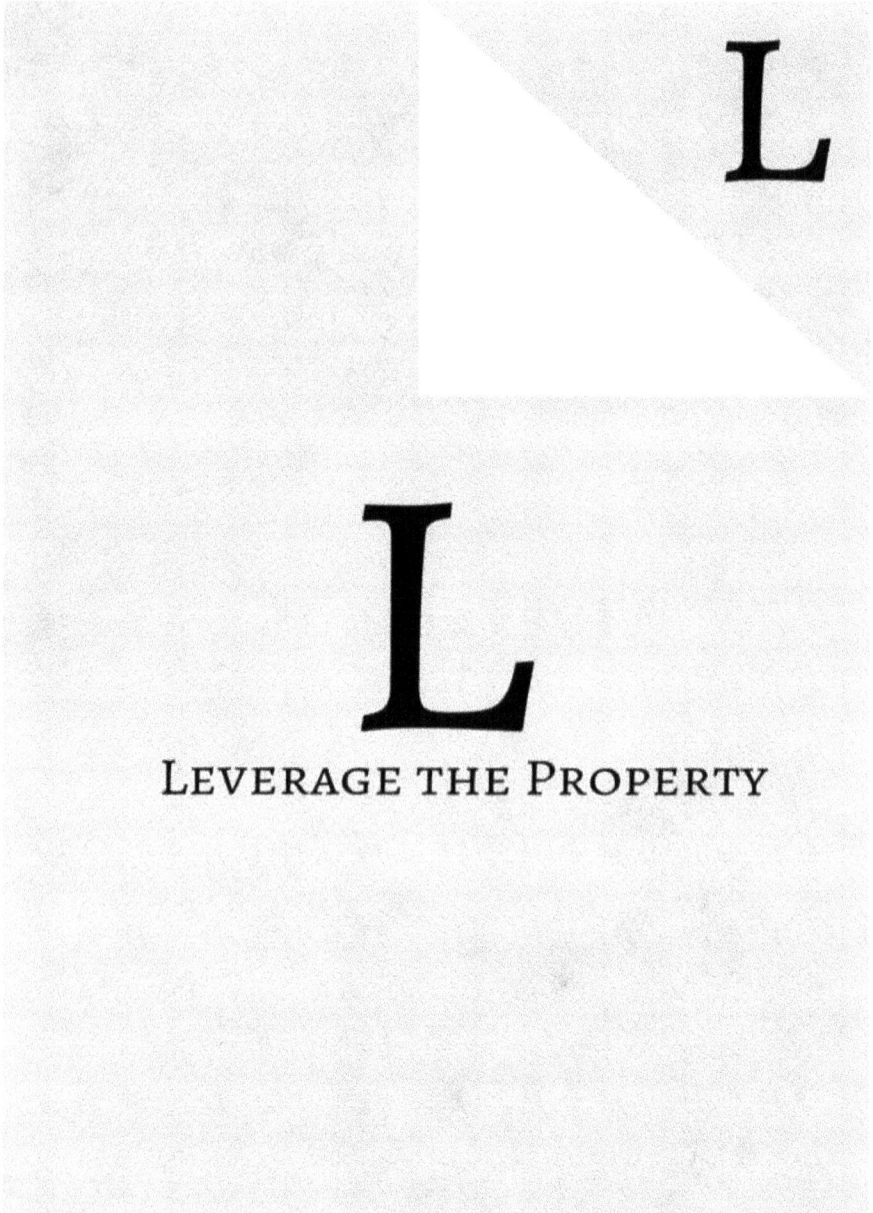

L

L

Leverage the Property

Chapter 4: LEVERAGING THE PROPERTY

"When we leverage, we aggregate and organize existing resources to achieve success." -Richie Norton

T he leveraging component of Real Estate investing, believe it or not, is where the separation between good and great investors begin—the funding of the deal. Getting the contract financed is the number one hindrance to new investors! Using my principles and the UnFair Academy strategies, makes it easier to acquire distressed properties, which ultimately become buy and hold, or fix and flip deals under contract.

Perhaps too easy, but what's next? Simply bragging on the fact, you have a house under contract for a $100,000 with an ARV of $200,000 means nothing, absolutely nothing, until you close it and the deal funds.

Find the Back Door First

Excuse me? Are you saying when I begin the inspection process to start at the back door? No! No! No! I'm talking about the exit strategy. Just like in elementary school, under state law, everyone knew—in case of fire—where the back door/fire exits were. Real Estate is no different.

In the normal flow of the business cycle, or in case of an emergency; know how you are going to get rid of the asset. The "back door" starts with the goal or purpose of the property. What is the goal of this property? Is it a fix and flip, buy and hold, rental property, or a wholesale piece? Hmmm...

Leveraging the property first starts with the "back door" of the property in mind. What's the exit? Getting to the purpose of the property begins with an evaluation of the property. Project items to consider:

- How much work is involved in the renovation?

- How long will that work take?

- Maintenance issues i.e., plumbing, roof, or foundation problems that may need addressing.

These assessments play an essential role in determining which leverage option to use that will save the most money. Remember, money saved here adds to the bottom line. Here are several financing methods that are used by investors.

Conventional Mortgage – very rarely, if ever, will a traditional conventional mortgage be used in leveraging a "fix & flip." Remember, we want distressed properties, in deplorable condition, barely livable. With a conventional mortgage, the lender's necessary prerequisites are the exact opposite. With 20% of the purchase price down, traditional conventional lenders provide fantastic rates. In turn, they require the property pass inspection and be in livable condition.

"Subject To" Investors Gold Mine!!!

"Subject To" – is an acquisition of title to real property upon which there is an existing mortgage, or deed of trust, where the new owner (you) agrees to take the title and the responsibility and continue to make the payments on the promissory note secured by a mortgage or deed of trust.

For a better understanding of how "Subject To" works, we must know within the purchase of all real estate, there are actually two separate transactions. First, is the signing of the deed/title. Second, is the signing of the mortgage/debt.

The deed is a formal document which states the legal owner of the real property. The mortgage is a promissory note to repay the debt incurred from the purchase of the deed. When buying a home "Subject To" the existing mortgage, in its purest form, means the buyer is not paying off the current mortgage and, therefore, in exchange for the transfer of ownership/deed/title of the real property, will continue to make the payments to the bank already associated with the mortgage on that property.

"Subject To" the existing loan is a very potent tool and should be one of the first questions asked in the fact-finding process. Don't be timid in asking and pushing for this type of financing from the seller; it will save thousands upon thousands on *every* transaction. Remember, the money made from saving money is an "art" in itself. You should practice it every chance you get.

What does this mean to you? How will a "Subject To" transaction benefit you? The advantages are on the next page.

1. No cash or credit is needed. – Since the loan is already in place, the only money paid at closing are minimal closing costs and any payment to the seller for the portion of equity out of the property.

2. Cheaper money. – Investment property interest rates are automatically higher than interest rates for homestead properties. The benefit is, getting an investment property at homestead property interest rates.

3. No unnecessary fees. – Since the property already has the mortgage in place, there is no need for a survey, appraisal, lender points, document prep, title policy, etc. Remember, money saved equals profit earned!

4. Total Autonomy. – If you can get the seller to finance the property "Subject To" the existing loan, it usually means the seller is flexible. The seller is basically handing over the keys to the car and saying, "You drive!" Which, in turn, means the ball is in your court. You get to name the title company, the date, and the time of the closing. All they want is their equity.

Hard Money

A loan based strictly on the value of the asset used explicitly in Real Estate to secure properties quicker and for a shorter duration of time. These loans have higher interests and origination fees. Usually, the money comes from an individual or a pool of investors. Using hard money is probably the most used form of leverage for fix and flips. The goal here is speed and efficiency.

For example, most hard money lenders will loan up to 75% of the ARV. Have a couple of hard money lenders on standby for every deal. Remember, unless you get a spectacular deal, expect to bring some cash to the closing table. The down payment you bring will often be for closing costs, repairs, and lender fees. The intent is to own the property for less than a year unless you become an "Accidental Landlord." If that happens, obviously you would want to refinance into a longer, more interest-friendly loan.

AcCiDeNtal Landlord

Owning a property where the initial purpose was to fix and flip. However, due to miscalculation, a shift in the market, and/or excessive inventory in the neighborhood, the price to achieve a profit could not be reached. Therefore, instead of selling it and taking a loss, it has now become a rental property with the intention of selling it when the market rebounds.

Don't be afraid of using hard money. Buying the property correctly, doing research on property values, and having a solid exit plan, this form of leveraging will be a tremendous tool in your arsenal.

There are a list of short-term and long-term financing options at http://www.UnfairAcademy.com if your desire is to buy and sell properties.

Private Money

A loan coming from an individual or a private institution not federally regulated is "private money." These loans have slightly higher interest rates than conventional banks, but, lower than hard money rates. There is less red tape, and credit issue allowances are more generous.

These loans are excellent for those who would not typically qualify for traditional lending. Like hard money, once you find a private money source, they are usually quick and efficient when it comes to closing.

Every serious investor needs a private money source. Earlier in the book, we established in order to answer or to solve a question; we must know these three components:

- *How?*

- *When?*

- *Why?*

For private money, we must ask:

- *Who has the money?*

- *Why should they lend to you?*

- *How does it benefit you?*

Who Has the Money?

How do people get money to invest? Hmmm, let me guess… Be a neurosurgeon in practice for several years; that will do the trick, for sure. But, other than that, below is a list of occupations that traditionally pay high salaries and provide extra cash to invest passively in real estate. They include:

A. Lawyers – personal injury or medical malpractice, civil cases, or class action suits. (They have 7-figure paydays)

B. Senior Level Management – Corporate CEO's, CFO's, or

CIO's of large publicly traded companies.

C. Retirees – Individuals with large 401k or IRA accounts.

D. Silver Spooners – Trust fund babies or estate beneficiaries.

E. Former Investors – Individuals who have sold their portfolios.

F. Entrepreneurs – Those who are looking to find multiple streams of monthly income.

G. Happy Go Lucky's – Lottery winners.

Do you know any of them? If so, ask to set up a potential business meeting. At first, they may be skeptical (remember, they are extremely smart people); however, over time, as your portfolio grows, they may be willing to take interest (pardon the pun) in investing with you. Here's why.

Why Should They Lend to You?

Amongst the obvious, to get paid from the interest. Here are more reasons why being on the lending side of private money is so attractive:

A. Better return rates than the stock market;

B. Money every month from the investment; and,

C. Possibly always wanted to be in Real Estate, but never had the time or pursued the knowledge of the industry.

How Does It Benefit You?

A. Lower rates than hard money;

B. Quicker closings;

C. No "red tape" and less documentation, as the asset is the leverage.

D. If the private money lender has money, deals are limitless;

E. Not credit score driven.

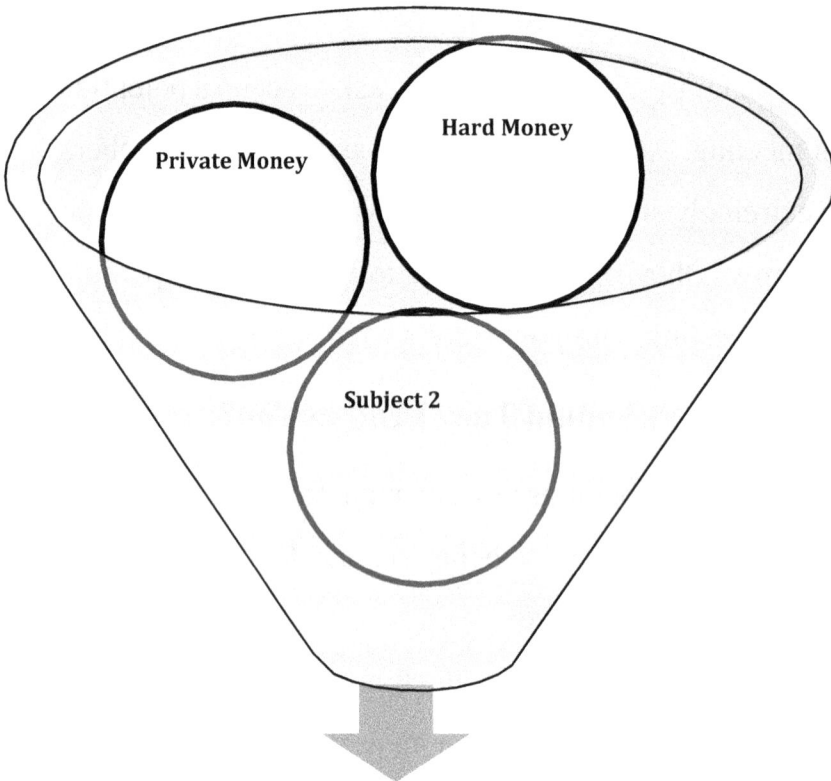

I

I

Improve The Property

Chapter 5: IMPROVING THE PROPERTY

T his chapter will be short and sweet. Mainly because improving it is based more on personal flavor, as opposed to hard rules and steadfast principles.

If we are honest with ourselves, we would love the opportunity to eat at our favorite steakhouse, seafood, or Mexican restaurant every night. However, often, we end up supporting our local Wendy's, McDonald's, or Subway. Why? What's the difference? Our favorite restaurants' food quality is superior, the atmosphere is more suitable for dining, and there's even a wait staff that brings our meal. The determining factor between the two is simple, the cost!

Remember this number: **18.** Yes, 18% of the potential profit is tied to how efficient (both time and money) the property can be improved. Along with the pure cost of the project, there is at least one more skill to master: The ability to assess the cost of the renovation accurately. It is a must that you learn how to determine the costs of the renovation. Here are some of the factors to calculate:

1. **Materials** – Basic flooring, paint, fixtures, and cabinetry are natural staples in a renovation process. However, don't forget to add the little things, such as tape and bedding, paintbrushes, floor padding, grout, mortar, etc. Remember, they cost too.

2. **Labor** – Consider the level of expertise and what you are willing to pay. Here is the ultimate dilemma… should I go all out, should I be conservative, where is the middle ground? Whatever your flavor of choice, calculate accordingly.

3. **Time** – Yes, time equals money. There are "carrying costs" for each Real Estate flip. They may not be as blatant and upfront as material, labor, and supplies, but they do affect the bottom line. Mortgage payments, insurance, taxes, electricity, gas, and water accrue daily.

Now, it's time to get your hands dirty and begin the process of improving your investment. Improving the property, just like leveraging, requires knowledge of the plan of the "back door."

Rehab Cost

The most challenging aspect of flipping is finding a small investment property that needs limited repairs to reach the full ARV. Smaller properties are the best project for newbie investors. No matter the size of the house, a budget must still be set. My college professor once uttered, "You don't have to be smart to graduate; just be organized." The same principle applies here.

> *You have taken on a new job title; it is now "Manager." Your job description is simple: To be on time and within the budget.*

Use a budget repair form, or an excel spreadsheet, to itemize each repair. Some of the line items on your repair form should have a space for how much it cost and how long it should take. After adding up all the figures, you should arrive at the final budget and estimated timeframe for completion. I always have the final budget at the forefront of my mind as the project is flowing. The final budget is important; it is a direct contributor to the bottom line. Be disciplined and stick to it.

Building Your Team

Most contractors would love only doing the repair work. But the reality is, they are 50% contractor and 50% business marketers. Ask yourself would you take a small discount in salary to work from home and not have to be in traffic or pay for gas. Contractors are no different; they would prefer to drive to a project, work the hours necessary, go home, and repeat the process the next day. However, a contractor must do the advertising, marketing, and drive around bidding on jobs they have a one in ten chance of securing the bid. It is very time consuming and not to mention frustrating. How much of a discount would the contractor give to you knowing 50% of their other job description is now eliminated? Find that sweet spot and massage it to the max! Doing this will benefit both parties involved.

Make It Fun and Efficient!

Make it easy; make it fun and make it efficient for your contractors. How can you do that? Use the same list of colors, materials, and supplies. I keep it simple. For big-ticket items, make a list of SKU numbers for the countertops, hardwood flooring, and carpet. This saves time ordering materials and being efficient in knowing where in the store the materials are located.

Making it easy and suitable for your contractors helps you as well. Let me explain. Since you have a mental blueprint of the renovation, when you walk through the property during the renovation, you know precisely the stage of the process. The additional benefit of using the same color in paints, material, and supplies is there will always be leftover materials. Save them; put them in storage for your next flip, as this will save you money. Thus, increasing your bottom line on the next one.

From the Inside-Out

When most of my friends and fellow contractors start the rehab process, they start from the exterior and move to the interior.

I emphatically disagree! Once the rehab starts, always—I mean always—begin from the interior and move to the exterior. Here is why!

There are nosey people in this world, especially neighbors. (Can I get an "Amen"?) If you start the renovation process from the outside to the inside, there will be noise from the construction and other distractions that will cause them (the nosey folks) to stop by and be nosey. When they do, (as most folks will,) they will want to see the interior of the property. Guess what? The interior is a mess. Here is what it would look like: There is no flooring; the pipes are exposed; the old, nasty refrigerator is still there; bathroom toilets haven't been flushed in weeks, and the odor from the previous owners' filthy dog or cat can be smelled upon entry. Get my drift?

It will be hard for them to see the "potential" of the property, and more importantly, they won't give you "free advertising" to their friends who might be interested in living closer to them based on those negative results. You are a smart person; you've bought the book, start from the inside and move to the outside. I hope you heed this caution.

Don't Forget the Kitchen and Bathrooms

When a woman enters a home she may potentially purchase, she walks straight to the kitchen. The flooring, the colors of the bedroom, and even the size of the master bedroom closet does not matter if you don't go *"all in"* on the kitchen and bathrooms.

Spend a good portion of your total rehab budget here. Ensure that your color schemes, tile, countertops, and backsplash are up to the quality within the price point you are seeking to achieve. If there is a portion of the kitchen that is *curable functional obsolescence* then, attack the

issue and get it right. It is that important.

Curable functional Obsolescence

Is measured in the cost to "cure" or rehab the functional obsolescence. Ex. If the kitchen is outdated, needs more space, or plumbing rearrangements; Will spending the money "cure/rehabbing" be outweighed by the potential profit to be made. If so, then the functional obsolescence is curable. (i.e., If it cost $10,000 to fix, but it will add $35,000 to the profit, equals curable.)

Your rehab task has a "Call to Action." Make every dollar count and spend the money where it counts most. My wisdom to you, it is usually found within these two rooms.

Curb Appeal

The function of great curb appeal for you is simple. It is to attract drive-thru traffic and to increase the emotional value of the property. Remember, your goal is to have several buyers bidding on your property. Curb appeal falls under the category of perceived value, which doesn't have to be expensive. What's the best way to pre-judge the inside of a residence? Have a stellar outside appeal. When people buy, they are looking for the maximum potential of the property. Create the visual that adds emotional value; it will add to your objective of increasing your profit.

The last part about the improvement process has nothing to do with contractors. It's having a trusted Real Estate agent on your team. Don't use just any realtor; use one who has specific expertise in that neighborhood. They should know the desires of potential buyers of said neighborhood.

Although this may seem small, however, trust me on this, it works. Think about it; simply adding a fancier fixture, a brighter color scheme, or different floor pattern ($200 extra cost) can catch the eye of the buyer and raise the "emotional value" of the property significantly.

DETAILS, DETAILS, DETAILS

"Remember details matter too. They create depth that touches the emotional soul"- B.Octavius Fair

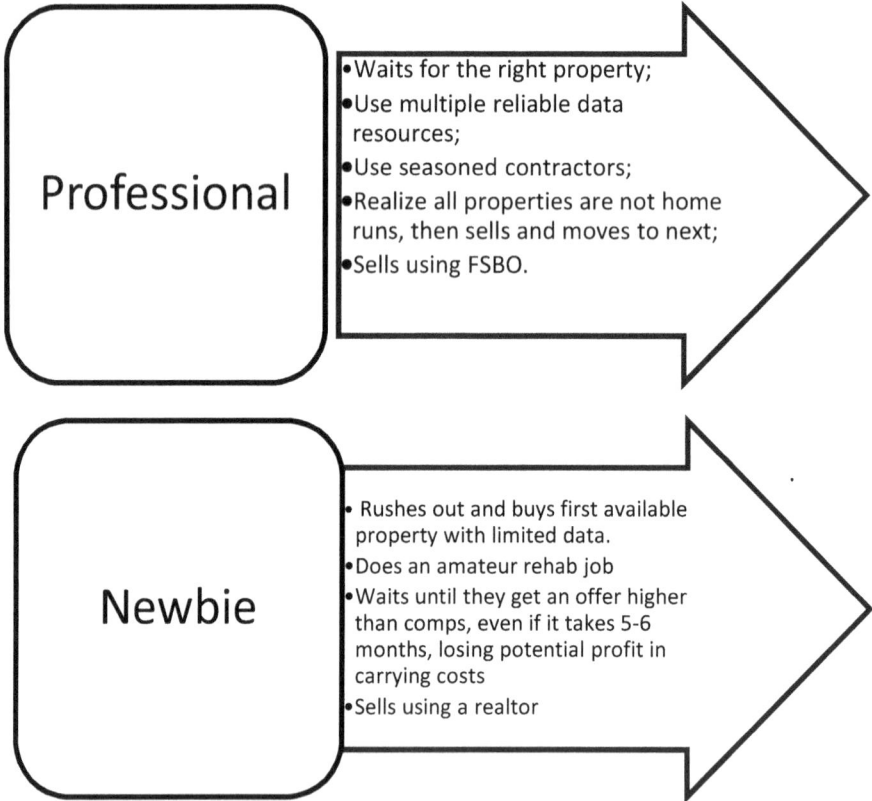

Professional
- Waits for the right property;
- Use multiple reliable data resources;
- Use seasoned contractors;
- Realize all properties are not home runs, then sells and moves to next;
- Sells using FSBO.

Newbie
- Rushes out and buys first available property with limited data.
- Does an amateur rehab job
- Waits until they get an offer higher than comps, even if it takes 5-6 months, losing potential profit in carrying costs
- Sells using a realtor

06

PROFITING FROM IT

06

P

P

Profit From The Property

Chapter 6: PROFITING FROM THE PROPERTY

> *"It's not how much money you make, but how much you keep, how hard the money works for you, and how many generations you keep it for."*
>
> *Robert Kiyosaki*

Turning a profit will ultimately keep you in business. If this statement is true, then obviously, your objective is to maximize this effort. The difference between good and great profits come from correct evaluation, calculation, and execution. We want big fat checks; we should leave no stone unturned and use every available resource to secure our profit. Why am I stressing this point? Why is this so important? Three words, "Loss opportunity cost."

When we leave "money on the table" by not maximizing our profit, it is never the dollar amount we initially lost or did not gain; it is significantly more. Here is why. The reality is you have lost the "opportunity" to have invested that money into more projects. A $7000 loss of potential profit could have been turned into \$50,000 in a short period of time using the right investment vehicle.

When we think of making a profit, we often calculate what we paid for it, then set a nominal price above that number. Making a profit sounds like the easy part; however, in reality, it's the most intellectual and challenging aspect of F.L.I.P.—no wonder it's the last letter: "P."

Price the Home Correctly

What is the maximum price for which the house will sell in a reasonable amount of time? What is the average "Days on the Market" (DOM) for this neighborhood? Is it too late in the seasonal selling cycle? These factors are essential in getting the most money for your property.

Overpricing a property will inflate the DOM. Remember, the "carrying cost clock" continues to tick, which flows contrary to your profit. *Ouch!* Also, overpricing may eventually force a price reduction. If this happens, buyers become skeptical and begin to wonder why the property has been discounted.

When this happens, they are not impressed enough to move forward. Listing a property too low, you will be inundated with tons of offers; thus, having to go back to the "drawing board" and asking for "Best and Final" offers which takes even more time.

Murphy's Law

After weeks of scheduling projects and rehabbing, you finally arrived at the point where you feel comfortable to place the home on the market. From the naked eye, it seems easy as 1, 2, and 3. First, list the house on the MLS. In less than a week, there is a buyer. The buyer is willing to pay at or near the listed price, then the negotiations begin—back and forth, back and forth, until finally the contract is signed. The deal is sent to the title company, and now you are waiting to get paid!

That's how the process should go, "Excuse Me," says Murphy's Law—meaning whatever can go wrong, will go wrong. That's just life in the world we live in, and sometimes we can't get around it. Because we are humans, there will be uncertainty and some delays, even in the absolute best of circumstances, so be prepared.

Listing on the MLS is the most effective way to sell the property, even if it "usually" (I'll explain later…) costs 6% of the selling price. That said, it (the MLS) does provide the absolute best way to market your property to bona fide buyers.

Since the goal is to make huge profits, the absolute best

way to secure those profits is by saving on the expenses associated in the selling process. Believe it or not, there are ways to protect your potential earnings even at this stage of the process.

To start the process of working with a realtor or a broker, a listing agreement must be signed. A listing agreement is a contract between a real estate broker and an owner of real property. This agreement grants the realtor the authority to act as the owner's "agent" in the sale of the property. Amongst other things stated in this contract, the listing agreement will state the fees charged by the realtor/broker.

Before you zero in on an agent to handle this transaction, have a conversation about the listing agreement. Most people are accustomed to negotiating the price of a car, price of a house, or even jewelry, so why not negotiate the cost of the listing agreement?

Strike a deal on the listing agreement, here is how. Offer a Flat Fee Listing. Flat Fee Listing is a proposed set amount not based on a percentage. This arrangement needs to be in the contract and agreed upon by both the selling agent and buyers' agent.

If the home is priced correctly, it should move fast without much work from the realtors.

TRADITIONAL MLS LISTING FEE VS FLAT FEE LISTING	
TRADITIONAL MLS LISTING FEE	
SELLING PRICE	$185,000
BUYER'S AGENT (3%)	$ 5,550
SELLER'S AGENT (3%)	$ 5,550
NET TO YOU	**$173,900**
FLAT LISTING FEE	
SELLING PRICE	$185,000
FLAT FEE(.0475)	8,787.5
NET TO YOU	**$176,212.5**
PROFIT OF	2,312.5

Listing Agreement

There are ways to add power to the negotiations with your realtor. They are found in the listing agreement. Implement these provisions:

1. The listing agreement should only be 60 days (worst-case scenario 90 days). The agent will likely ask for 180 days, which is entirely too long and slanted completely his/her way. My approach is to always create a sense of urgency. A 180-day listing agreement does the exact opposite.

2. Insert a buyout provision that enables you to pay

the agent a fee for the marketing and advertising dollars that may have been spent in the event you find a buyer on your own. A buyout provision puts the agent on notice you are actively trying to sell the property as well. The agent will realize there is instant competition with even greater detail of the product (the house) being sold... *YOU!*

Inside the Contract

It is understood by the signing of the contract; there is an agreement on the selling price. However, in every single- family residential closing, there are costs the title company charges for servicing the transaction. These items are stated on the HUD 1 statement and can also be negotiated upon the signing of the contract. We call it "The Inside of the Contract."

Things "inside of the contract" can generate profit as well. Some of the items most sellers customarily innately inherit (i.e. closing cost, title policy, and survey) are an absolute **"NO-NO"** in my business model. In all my negotiations, I always start by instructing the buyer to pay all closing costs($1000), title policy (roughly 1% of purchase price), and the survey ($475). *No EXCEPTIONS!* Now, whether I achieve my goal of going 3-0 in getting all my request granted is one thing; often, we usually settle somewhere in the middle. But the key is, do not be afraid to ask. If you have priced the home correctly, do not be fearful of losing any buyer based upon the "inside of the contract." Remember, you have invested the time, energy, and money in this project, at least be proud enough to ask!

Maximizing the Profits Recap

1. Price. Price. Price. – Price the property correctly the *first* time; don't let the market do it!

2. Flat Listing Fee – 4.75%

3. Limit listing agreement to 60-days.

4. Buyout clause if the seller finds the buyer independently.

5. Inside the contract, make it work to your advantage.

6. Offer a home warranty.

7. Get the buyer to the table

<u>NOTES</u>

Call 2 Action

I hope I've provided enough information for you to begin your real estate investing career. If this is true, help me to help others be more successful. Spread the word! You can:

- Like my page on Facebook (BOCTAVIUS);

- Post about the book like crazy on Twitter and Instagram; and,

- Write a fantastic book review on either of the above, plus Amazon.

I've presented a lot of material, and some would attest too much information. I genuinely believe in helping others, help themselves. I know being successful in Real Estate is indeed possible and life changing. Heck, look at me; I've done it. I didn't come from money nor fame. It all started with a dream and going to the *right* person who had the *correct* information.

Even in that initial dream, I was smart enough to know I needed a mentor. I wanted to be great and, throughout history, all the great individuals have had someone who guided them to and through greatness. Michael Jordan had a coach, Muhammed Ali had a trainer;

heck, the great Warren Buffet has a few financial managers on his team even now. Why not you? The most important step is the very next step: **STARTING YOUR JOURNEY**. But how you start is more crucial than anything else.

Starting can be tricky, and if not done correctly, will lead to early frustration and ultimately quitting. Here's where I can aid and navigate you through starting correctly. I want to be your personal coach and mentor. Sign up at **<u>BOCTAVIUS.COM</u>,** and let's get moving together. I would love to have an opportunity to help you change your life.

**BONUS
MATERIAL**

<u>NOTES</u>

Chapter 7: BONUS MATERIAL

Characteristics of A First Flip

In this aspect, everyone is the same; we like to brag and boast of all the incredible accomplishments we have made. Real Estate investing can humble you. Ever heard of the show "Flip or Flop?" By the title alone indicates all deals are not "home runs," and suggests there are some failures in this business. In this chapter, I must confess and be completely transparent.

After being in the industry for quite some while, there were some transactions I wish I wouldn't have made. Unfortunately for me, I didn't have a guide/coach/mentor to help me maneuver through the do's and don'ts of real estate investing. But, fortunately for you, you have this book and the UnFair Academy to navigate through the "minefields" of real estate investing.

There is no magic formula or blueprint that will solve all the mistakes that can be potentially made. However, to help you get started on the "right foot,"

113

here are some of the characteristics of your first investment property.

> **Size-1500-1800 sq. ft.**
>
> **Price range 85,000-160,000**
>
> **Location-Neighborhood built 1990- 1999**
>
> **Type of neighborhood-Middle class**
>
> **Repairs needed- 30-45k**
>
> **One story**

A three bedrooms, two baths, 1500-1800 sq. ft., with a garage home will offer more than enough challenge to begin your flipping experience. Houses of this size are a perfect match for your rehab budget. Here are reasons why:

1. **Buying material** – only limited to 1500-1800sq ft. of materials. (i.e. flooring and paint)

2. **Getting estimates from contractors** – Most contractors charge per square foot (between $1-$3 per ft.), so obviously cost will be maxed out at 1800 sq. ft.

3. **Overflow allowance** – Overflow allowance is for any unforeseen miscellaneous expenditures that may arise from error or oversight. Again, it is limited to the max of 1800sq ft. Here's an example.

Conceptualize this: You did every imaginable inspection before you bought the property and never pulled up the carpet. Underneath the padding is a foundation crack one inch wide and nine feet long. (Hopefully, for you, it's just limited to this one room.) If the damages are extensive, they are limited to a max 1800 square feet.

A house of this size is a perfect match for selling.

Invariably, I operate from the mindset to always be in a position of strength, power, and demand. Buying and rehabbing a 1500-1800 sq. ft., 3-bed, 2-bath one-story house with a garage fits all three categories: Position of Strength, Power, and Demand. Let me explain.

1. **The Strength** – a 3-bed, 2-bath single-family residence will always be a staple in the United States housing market. It makes up 45% of the housing industry's inventory.

2. The Power – Because of the price point ($105k-$200k pending metroplex), there is power when it comes to negotiating the selling of your investment. You will have multiple offers and the flexibility in raising the prices due to the demands for the house.

3. **The Demands** – A three-bedroom, two-bath, one-story with a garage residence is a first-time homeowner's dream. Something not so small that they can still grow into it, and not so large they can't furnish it. The size and price are very accommodating to marginal credit buyers. Also, a three-bedroom, two-bath, one-story house is the perfect size for those older Americans who now have an "empty nest." They are now downsizing from a two-story to a one-story due to space and age (climbing stairs at 65 years old is not ideal), this property will accommodate perfectly.

Partnerships

Remember my initial goal to you? It is to provide the road of least resistance and to provide the optimum opportunity to succeed. In my real estate career, I must confess; I have never had a partner. I've always wanted total autonomy, especially when it came to money.

My words of wisdom to you, you should too. However, on some rare occasions, there will be an excellent deal that can't be passed up. The only way to make the deal happen is with the help of a partner. If this occurs, draft a joint venture agreement.

A joint venture is an entity, separate and apart from each participants' other business interests. It is very similar to a traditional business partnership, except for one key difference. A partnership, for the most part, is an ongoing and long-term business relationship.

A joint venture is a single business transaction. The main reason many investors choose this route is to share strengths, minimize risks, and increase competitive advantages.

Listed below are some types of traditional partnerships typically found in real estate.

117

Active Partnership

Active partnerships are, as the name would suggest, is when all partners put in equal money and equal time. The various tasks and daily functions are agreed upon and divided amongst equally. The end equity is distributed evenly.

Passive Partnership

The tasks are not equally divided. In its purest form, this is an arrangement where the private lender (passive partner) funds the entire deal and wants a portion of the equity at the end. In exchange for the private lender not charging an origination fee, interest on the loan during the duration of the rehab and requiring title insurance on the property. Once the property is sold, the passive partner (private lender) receives his/her portion of the "profit pie."

Sweat Equity Partnership

This arrangement would not be to split up the different tasks and daily functions. Instead, to make the split equal. One partner would bring all the money to closed, and for the rehab, the other partner would be responsible for completing all the repair work. The profit would be split based on the pre-arrangement between the partners.

Partnership Recap

I've heard horror stories about partnerships that consisted of two inexperienced investors. Since owning up to the total responsibility of a partnership can often be a burden, often, it hinders production, timing, and profit.

Keep in mind, the liability of each partner's debts of the business is limitless. Each partner is jointly and equally liable for all the partnership's debts. Simply stated, each partner is responsible for their share of partnership debts as well as debts incurred by the other partner. If you need money for your first flip, my advice would be, do not go in with a partner. Instead, borrow the money from a bank, friend, or family member with no strings attached other than (of course) the repayment. If you still can't raise enough cash to flip a property, consider wholesaling.

> *After all this flipping, one day you will want to retire.*
> *Wholesaling and flipping houses generate an*
> *enormous amount of "present day income." Residual*
> *income and net worth are now needed to*
> *become wealthy.*

Building Your Real Estate Empire

Once you have become a successful wholesaler or a flipper, it is imperative you invest your fortunes back into your business. One of the most popular ways to re-invest is to have a single-family residential real estate portfolio.

I have a system in place where I buy in this format. I wholesale a property and earn a fee between $7k-$15k. I then use the earned fee to purchase a home for the sole purpose of flipping the property. I flip that property and make a profit between $35k-$50k. Then, I take the proceeds from the flipped property and use it as a down payment for a rental investment property. The rental property produces a cash flow of $450-$500 per month. I rinse and repeat that process.

Most of my friends and colleagues are strictly wholesalers and flippers. However, to me, building a rental property portfolio over time is more profitable, efficient, and thus more sustainable than buying and selling over shorter periods of time. Here are my reasons why:

1. **Capital Gains Taxes** – From the properties you sell, you must pay taxes on the profit/gain. I'm not a CPA or a tax attorney, so check your local and federal guidelines for the tax rate for capital gains. But, the one thing I do know is they (the taxes) are high.

2. **Selling can be expensive.** – Although you are making a profit from the selling of your property, the fees from realtors, title work, surveys, and closing costs can rack up rather quickly.

3. **Money, Money, Money** – Because you have it, you are more susceptible to spending it. It is very tempting to spend it on depreciable assets and frivolous living. In six months to a year from now, if you don't have a solid business plan and/or great discipline, you will have nothing to show for your marvelous work… only stories.

121

4. Net Worth – Over time, when tenants continue to pay rent, three things are always moving in concert. Your mortgage balance with the bank goes down. Your property value appreciates. And, lucky you, you get paid cashflow monthly. All these factors contribute to your net worth rising over time.

While the priorities of building a Real Estate portfolio starts with the acquisition of the first one, we must think globally about your entire business model. The order of the day should always encompass these two things: The preservation of the capital invested, and to make a decent return on the investment.

Make sure the property will maintain its worth for at least five-to-seven years after a 30-year note has been satisfied. Buy homes in areas where the middle class will always live. Stay away from high crime areas and places that are undesirable. While in general, over time, all houses appreciate, homes in high crime areas and undesirable neighborhoods don't appreciate as well as other neighborhoods.

> *"A wise man learns from the mistakes of others;*
>
> *a fool learns from his own."-Otto von Bismarck*

10 Mistakes NOT to Make!

1. *Money is made when you buy, not when you sell!*

Although this is a statement, it can be one of the biggest mistakes made. The ARV is the ARV. No matter how much work you put into the property, it is extremely hard to change the intrinsic value of a neighborhood.

There are some ways to add some value, like adding an additional bathroom, bedroom, garage, or even a pool, but you are spending money, *hoping* to get it back. The surest way to ensure a property makes money is on the front end. The price point where you bought the property. Do everything within your power to buy at a point wherein the worst-case scenario, you still make a profitable payday.

2. *Never pay a down payment to contractors to "start" work.*

Where else in America do you get paid **before** you complete the job? Go to the doctor; get billed afterward. Go to the supermarket; pay at the register. What about your favorite restaurant? Nope, not there either. The tab comes after you have *finished* dining. Nowhere else, so why here? The "money" should always be behind the work.

Example: From the contractors' estimation, the job should take one week. The payments should resemble this… work Monday and Tuesday, get paid Tuesday evening for Monday's work. Get the point?

This is a tale-tell sign of the quality of the contractor. If they don't accept your terms, walk away. I promise the longer you are in the business, the more horror stories you will hear of contractors burning off with your hard-earned money.

3. *Not buying your own materials.*

Giving a contractor money to purchase materials will simply get you the cheapest materials at the highest

124

price. Controlling your costs starts here. Most stores allow you to buy online and sometimes will even deliver to the worksite.

4. *Working too far from home.*

We must always remember the value and the importance of time. Having a rehab project far away from your home or business burns time and energy just simply driving to the project. Treating this like a corporate job, most of us wouldn't travel 50 miles one way to work every day.

I like to micromanage and stay on top of the work. I'm at the worksite three or four times a day. It would be impossible to drive that many miles per day. Find an investment property within a 15-20-minute drive from your home or your office. It will undoubtedly make a big difference at the pump and increase your overall productivity and efficiency as well.

5. *Not planning before you close.*

Again, time is money... Get the "scope work" done before closing. Measurements, materials, and contractors should be in place the same day of closing.

6. *Closing later in the day and not in the morning.*

The clock is ticking; taxes begin the day of closing. Why not get your full day's money worth? Although it may seem small, this builds discipline in watching each dollar, thus maximizing your profit potential.

7. *Not getting an LLC.*

Before the bell rings in every boxing match, the referee says, "Protect yourself at all times." Having your properties deeded into an LLC protects from being sued personally. All business debts, unless guaranteed by a personal guarantor, will fall into the LLC. If something were ever to go wrong or astray, the entity will be sued and not you personally. There are only a few legal documents that must be filed with the secretary of state in the state in which the LLC will be conducting business.

An LLC is more challenging to set up than a sole proprietorship or a partnership but knowing that some separation from business liabilities and personal liabilities is a must. Setting up and running an LLC is significant.

126

8. Stop having sub-par credit.

Get to know and improve your credit. Initially, you might not need it, but over time and indeed as your real estate investing career develops, it will become more and more vital. As you make money, take the time to further invest in yourself. Get your credit score above 720; it will pay off dividends in opening many more avenues of financing. Here is the information for the three major credit bureaus. Get on top of this right now!

TransUnion-www.Transunion.com
P.O. Box 1000 Chester, PA 19022 (800)-916-8800

Experian – www.Experian.com
P.O. Box 4500 Allen, TX 75013 (888)-397-3742

Equifax – www.Equifax.com
P.O. Box 740241 Atlanta, GA 30374-0241 (800)-685-1111

9. Getting frustrated too soon

Be sure to align your expectations with the amount of time, energy, and effort you put in. Work only 30 minutes to one hour per week and expect *those* results. Work 40-50 hours per week and *expect* those results. Remember, frustration only comes in when expectations are out of line.

10. *Not buying title insurance-* Always make sure the TITLE is marketable. The deed shows evidence of ownership; however, it is not the complete picture. The title is PROOF of ownership. You need this assurance. The title company is willing to insure that once all closing documents are signed, you are the only one who can claim ownership of the property. It is very challenging chasing down deceased people looking for their signatures, and virtually impossible to locate their heirs. Save the time, buy the insurance.

Final Thoughts

Mark Twain said it best, "The best two days of your life are the day you were born, and the day you figured out why." Figuring out your purpose and living out your financial dream can both be accomplished in Real Estate. Making a lot of money in Real Estate involves countless hours of dedication and focus. There is a commitment level that is not for the faint of heart.

Being successful in Real Estate involves excellent decision-making skills for identifying great deals and life choices in general. Here is my theory:

When we decide, we are killing one or more of the other options. When we say *yes* to a right turn, we are saying *no* to a left turn. When we say *yes* to wearing jeans and a tee-shirt, we are saying *no* to wearing a suit. In a sense, the other options die and fall by the wayside. The same can hold true to investing in Real Estate.

When you say *yes* to investing in Real Estate, you are saying *no* and killing off the other options, such as buying depreciable items, wasting time procrastinating, and having poor credit. We must change our mental attitude and start saying *yes* to building good credit—*yes*, to starting a rental

129

portfolio, and *yes,* to reaching back and helping others gain the same financial freedom you are attempting to attain. There is plenty of money to be made in Real Estate. Have an in-depth conversation with yourself, encourage yourself, and know that others have achieved great success! Why not you?

Facts and Stats

There is an abundance of work and plenty of money to be made. Here are some facts and stats to support it.

- In the first half of 2018, house flippers made an average gross return of 44.3% or $65,250 per deal. – ATTOM Data.
- In the fourth quarter of 2018, 10.9% of all homes sold were flips. – CoreLogic

The National Average rate of return for an investment rental property is 11.5%. The average length of time to flip a property:

A. Experienced Flipper: 90-120 Days.

B. Some Experience: 120-180 Days.

C. First Flip: 150-210 Days.

National Average costs for the total rehab project is $49,750. National Average percentage rate for hard money is 13.75%.

The National Average for origination points for Hard Money 3%.

According to CNBC's "Make It" the top states for flipping houses are: Tennessee (TN), Pennsylvania (PA),

New Jersey (NJ), Louisiana (LA), Colorado (CO), Maryland (MD), Virginia (VA), Florida (FL), Illinois (IL), and Kentucky (KY).

5.34 million existing homes were sold in 2018 – National Association of REALTORS®

There are approximately 121.6 million occupied housing units in the United States. The typical home size is 1,500 square feet. All according to the 2017 American Housing Survey.

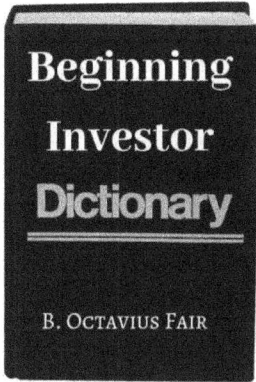

Investor Dictionary

Beginning Investor Dictionary

B. OCTAVIUS FAIR

Here are the most commonly used words for a new to intermediate investor. Get to know them.

A

Acceleration clause
A clause in your mortgage which allows the lender to demand payment of the entire outstanding loan balance. The contract performance is "accelerated," when the agreed-upon circumstances are triggered. Some of the conditions that trigger the acceleration are the death of a borrower, transfer of title to another individual, or simply defaulting on the payment of the loan.

Acquisition Cost
The price and total fees associated with obtaining a property.

Acre
A measure of land equaling 4,840 square yards or 43,560 square feet.

Appreciation
Increase in the value of a property over time

Assessed value

The valuation placed on real property by a public tax assessor for purposes of taxation. Some of the factors it considered are comparable home sales, age of property, depreciation, and current condition of the property.

Assignee

The person an agreement or contract is transferred or sold to.

Assignment

The method a contract is transferred by/to.

Assignor

The person who assigns an agreement or contract to the assignee.

Assumable mortgage

An assumable mortgage is an alternative type of financing arrangement where the outstanding mortgage and all its terms are transferred from the current owner to a new buyer. By assuming the current owner's remaining debt, the buyer can avoid having to obtain a new mortgage; usually, there are some qualifying standards the buyer must meet before this type of financing is approved.

B

Bond market

Usually refers to the daily buying and selling of thirty-year treasury bonds. Mortgage lenders follow this market because as the yields of bonds fluctuate, fixed-rate mortgages do the same.

C

Capitalization rate, or "cap rate." A formula used to determine the value of an investment. The Cap rate percentage is arrived by dividing the total net operating income of the asset by the current value of the asset.

Cash flow
The flow of money in and out of a business or property.

Cash flow property
A surplus in revenue generated each month after all expenses have been paid.

Contingency
 A condition that must be met before a contract is legally binding. (Illustration: I must sell my house first, then buy the new property.

Cost of funds index (COFI)
One of the indexes that are used to determine interest rate changes for certain adjustable-rate mortgages. It represents the weighted-average cost of savings, borrowings, and advances of the financial institutions such as banks and savings & loans in the 11th District of the Federal Home Loan Bank.

D

Debt Coverage Ratio (DCR)
A ratio used for underwriting purposes. It is arrived by dividing net operating income by total debt service. Most investors strive for 1.20 or higher.

Draw
 A periodic advance of funds from a lender. Usually, from hard money or private investor.

E

Earnest Money

Money is given to the seller, by a buyer, to show good faith that the property will be purchased.

Eminent domain

The right of a government to take private property for public use upon payment of its fair market value.

Encumbrance

Anything that affects or limits the fee simple title to a property, such as mortgages, leases, easements, or restrictions.

Equity

It is the difference between the current market value of a property and the amount owed by the owner, which includes all mortgages, taxes, and/or liens against the property.

Examination of title

The report on the title of a property from the public records or an abstract of the title.

F

Flood insurance

Insurance that compensates for physical property damage resulting from flooding. It does require the property to be in a Federal designated flood area.

Functional obsolescence

A reduction of a home's usefulness or desirability due to it having an outdated design feature that cannot be easily changed.

HUD – 1 Statement

HUD refers to the Department of Housing and Urban Development. A form used by a title company or closing agent itemizing all charges to the borrower and seller in a real estate transaction. This form gives the total picture of the closing transaction.

J

Judicial Foreclosure

Judicial foreclosure proceedings on a property in which a mortgage lacks the power of sale clause and so proceeds through the courts. The power of sale is a clause written into a mortgage at the time of signing. This authorizes the mortgagee to sell the property in the event of default in order to repay the debt incurred from the mortgage.

L

Lease Back

Allows a buyer to rent the property back to the seller after closing, letting them stay in the home for a predetermined amount of time. (Usually less than 30- days.)

Line of credit

An agreement by a commercial bank or other financial institution to extend credit up to a certain amount for a specific time to a well-qualified borrower.

Liquid asset

Is cash or other assets that is easily converted into cash with a short period of time. Some examples of assets that fall into the "liquid assets" categories are money market instruments and market securities.

Loan servicing

After you obtain a loan, the company you make the payments to is "servicing" your loan. They process payments, send statements, manage the escrow/impound account, provide collection efforts on delinquent loans, ensure that insurance and property taxes are made on the property, handle pay-offs and assumptions, and provide a variety of other services.

Lock-in

An agreement in which the lender guarantees a specified interest rate for a certain amount of time at a particular cost.

Lock-in period

The time during which the lender has guaranteed an interest rate to a borrower.

M

Margin

The difference between the interest rate and the index on an adjustable-rate mortgage. The margin remains stable over the life of the loan. It is the index which moves up and down.

O

One Percent rule (1% Rule)

This refers to the rent to the expense ratio of an investment property to be profitable.

P

PITI

PITI is an acronym for Principal, Interest, Taxes, Insurance is the total sum of a mortgage payment that includes the principal amount, loan interest, property tax, and homeowner's property and if applicable, private mortgage insurance premiums.

PMI

PMI is short for Private Mortgage Insurance. Type of insurance mortgage lenders requires when homebuyers put down less than 20 percent of the home's purchase price. PMI protects lenders in case the homeowner defaults on the loan. PMI helps offset the lender's risk. In no way does PMI doesn't protect the buyer.

Power of Sale

The power of sale is a clause written into a mortgage note authorizing the mortgagee to sell the property in the event of default in order to repay the mortgage debt. The power of sale is permitted in many states as part of a lender's right to seek foreclosure.

R

Real Estate Owned or REO property

Property owned by a lender. Lenders generally take the title of the properties after not selling at a foreclosure auction.

Rehabilitation (Rehab)

Refers to the repairs needed to be done to improve the asset.

Rent loss insurance
Insurance that protects and reimburses the landlord for lost income due to fire or other casualties while the property is being repaired or rebuilt. In most cases, general property insurance itself doesn't cover lost rent while the property is being restored. During this time of repair or rebuilding, the tenant is excused from paying rent as the living conditions are not up to standards.

S

Self-Directed IRA (SDIRA)
A type of account that provides tax benefits or shelters to money deposited that is designated for retirement. Income from the account is taxed at the tax bracket the account holder reaches upon retirement. (The difference between a SDIRA and a typical IRA account is the type of investments the account holder is permitted to make.)

Single-family residence (SFR)
 A free-standing residential property designed to house one family.

T

Title Insurance
An insurance policy by the title company stating and protecting the current buyer and lender any and all previous liens or judgments against the property have been satisfied at the time of closing. Furthermore, it also implies at the time of closing that no one else can legally claim ownership of the property, except the insured.

Title search
A check of the title records by the title company to ensure the seller is the legal owner of the property and that there are no liens, judgments or other claims outstanding.

Truth-in-Lending

A federal law that requires lenders to fully disclose, in writing, the terms and conditions of a mortgage. Items that must be disclosed are the annual percentage rate (APR), closing documents, fees, and other charges.

Turnkey property

A property that has been purchased, rehabbed, and is ready to be rented or sold.

V

Vacancy Provision

Money set aside, or apart, by the owner for covering vacancy and maintenance. Usually, it is a percentage of the monthly rent. On average it is about 6% for vacancy and 6% for maintenance.

Y

Yield Spread Premium

Money paid to a mortgage broker for marking up the borrower interest rate. Often, it is paid in origination fees, broker fees, or discount points.

Acknowledgement and Special Thanks

T o the one above, the only true and living God, I'm thankful for the blessings you have continued to bestow upon me. I will continue to honor the gift(s) you have given to me by sharing with the world the good news that faithfulness, commitment, dedication, and sacrifice, in your Kingdom, will have its reward.

Special thanks to my beloved parents, Ruben Fair, and LaVena Lewis, I'm thankful for the nurturing and tutelage you have passed on to me throughout the years.

To the family that took me in as one of their own, The Wilkins: Rev, Phyllis, Hank V, and Wesley words can't express how your influence and the family infrastructure have shaped and sharpened my life. I am truly grateful!

To my best friend in the entire world, Marquis Alexander, your guidance and impact through this journey have made me the real estate investor/developer that I am today. Thanks a million (literally & figuratively).

To my best friend in heaven, Ronald "Tango" West, your voice of motivation and determination, and of course, your genuine and unique bass guitar skills I can still hear to this day, rest well, till we meet again, my brother.

I want to thank everyone that sacrificed their time, energy, and effort in making this book a reality. To my publisher, Johnny "Macknificent" Mack CEO/Founder of GetPublishedSuccessfully.com for inspiring me to write and share my accomplishments with the world. I'm grateful and thankful for your insight and knowledge of the world of authorship.

My editor in chief, Shaundale Rena thanks for polishing up my adult grammar skills, keep doing what you do, Let's write another one!!!!

Through my gift of music, God has allowed me to have several extended families. Special shout out to Highland Hills UMC (Pastor Hank Wilkins), my first church home.

To all of the rest of my church families , Saint James UMC Pine Bluff, El Bethel Baptist (Pastor Robert L. McKenzie and Justin Barker), Carver Heights Baptist(Pastor Daryl Carter), Keller Springs Baptist (Larry Sanders), Koinonia Baptist(Jerry Robinson), my current church home T.L.C. Fellowship(Pastor Tyrone Gordon), your excellent biblical exegesis, have made me the strong man of God I am today.

About the Author

B. Octavius Fair is a successful businessman, entrepreneur, father, motivational speaker, and leader. He discovered early on he had a natural propensity for sales and negotiations. Mr. Fair is a graduate of the prestigious Dallas Baptist University, where he earned a degree in Business Administration.

He leveraged that learned skillset into being a very highly compensated automobile salesperson. His intellectual prowess led him to begin to start investing in real estate.

Mr. Fair surreptitiously encountered a lucrative real estate deal and decisively took advantage of it, resulting in a handsome return on investment. For the next 20 months, Mr. Fair researched and engaged in the real estate market to great success.

During that learning period, he amassed a portfolio of over 5 million dollars and began teaching his efficacious skills to thankful individuals who sought his advice.

The success of his students led him to publish this book and be the founder of the UnFairAcademy.com. His products and materials are in demand all over the country. He looks forward to seeing you at one of his seminars, webinars, and other live events.

CONNECT

With B. Octavius Fair

SOCIAL
MEDIA

BOCTAVIUS- Facebook
BOCTAVIUS3247 - Instagram
@UNFAIRACADEMY - Twitter

EMAIL
INFO

BOCTAVIUS@BOCTAVIUS.COM
BOCTAVIUS@UNFAIRACADEMY.COM

WEBSITE

BOCTAVIUS.COM
UNFAIRACADEMY.COM

B. OCTAVIUS FAIR
REAL ESTATE INVESTOR   AUTHOR

www.ingramcontent.com/pod-product-compliance
Lightning Source LLC
Chambersburg PA
CBHW071838200326
41519CB00016B/4157